HAUNTED
EXETER

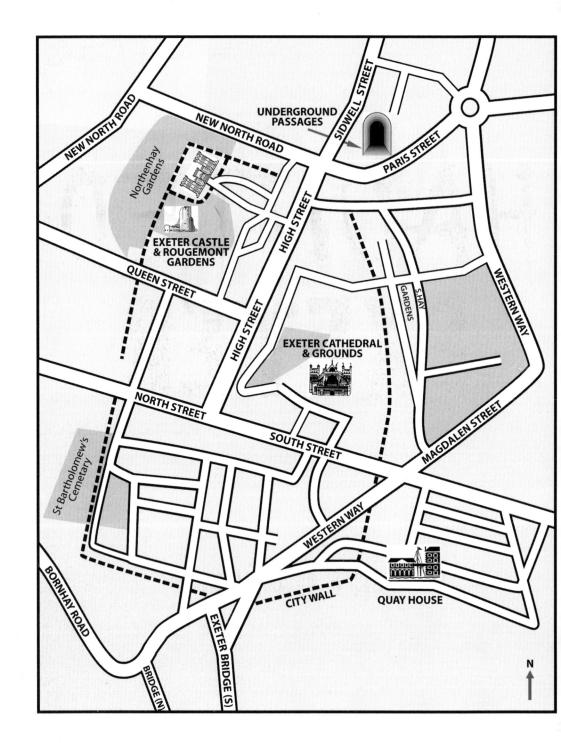

Exeter city centre

HAUNTED EXETER

Suze Gardner

The
History
Press

I would like to dedicate this book to Seal as thanks for his support and encouragement and for doing all the housework while I was writing

First published 2011

The History Press
The Mill, Brimscombe Port
Stroud, Gloucestershire, GL5 2QG
www.thehistorypress.co.uk

British Library Cataloguing in Publication Data.
A catalogue record for this book is available from the British Library.

ISBN 978 0 7524 5672 0
Typesetting and origination by The History Press
Printed in Great Britain

Contents

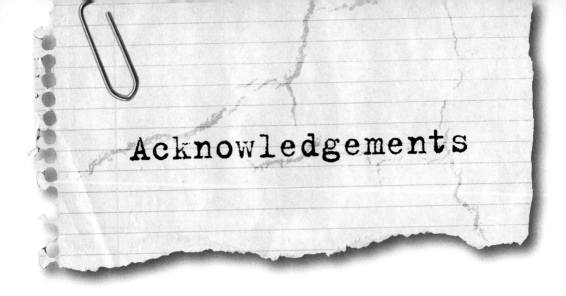

Acknowledgements

DURING the research and writing of this book I have had help and encouragement from many people. Some I have known for a long time, while some I met during the course of this work. I am fortunate that a number of these new acquaintances have now become firm friends.

I would like to extend special thanks to:

Linda Gibbons, Manager of Exeter Information and Tickets; Nina Corey and my colleagues at Exeter City Council; Colin Gale and his colleagues, the Exeter Redcoat guides; Tony Eccles, paranormal researcher, and Lee Rawlings, sound technician.

Chief Librarian Roger Brien, Devon and Exeter Institution; Peter Dawkes, Senior guide at Powderham Castle and Helen Dawkes; the staff at the Devon Record Office; staff of the Westcountry Studies Unit; Michael Evans, former General Secretary of the Exeter Spiritualist Church; George Wood; Jonathon Hill, spiritual healer.

Keely, Steve and Callie at the Cowick Barton Inn; Julian Wilkinson, Abode Hotels and staff at the Well House Pub; the White Hart Hotel; Julie and staff at the Barnfield Theatre; Kelli Melson, formerly of Lush Soaps; Mark, manager of the Ship Inn; Chris Park, Bowhill House; the staff of Pizza Express; Ernest Jones; Starz Bar; The Collection; Laura Ashley; Chevalier Inn and the numerous passers-by who kindly added little snippets of very useful information as I carried out my research.

Last but not least, thanks again to my partner Seal Faulkner, for putting up with the obsession I developed while researching *Haunted Exeter*.

I would like to thank Exeter City Council and Exeter Cathedral Library for the use of their pictures.

About the Author

SUZE Gardner is a historian, author and a playwright. She has lived in Devon for ten years. During this time she has researched Exeter's history and paranormal phenomena extensively, becoming fascinated by the way historical fact and ghost stories often come together in unexpected ways, each complemental to the other.

Introduction

I started writing about Exeter and its past as part of my job at the Exeter City Council where I began in tourist information, before moving on to work as a tour guide at the city's historic Underground Passages. I also helped as an Exeter Red Coat guide by running one of their very popular Halloween 'Spooks and Broomsticks' tours for several years. The experience I have gained has helped with the writing of *Haunted Exeter* immensely.

A free easy to use full-colour map of the city centre produced by Exeter City council is available from Exeter Visitor Information and Tickets and other venues. The map is split into separate quarters (meaning 'areas' rather than actual 'quarters' as there are more than four) Since the map is laid out in a manner which has proved helpful to visitors and locals alike, it seemed logical to use the same layout in this book. Areas of the city outside the centre can easily be explored using any street map.

Exeter is a wonderful place for a historian to write about. Firstly, the city has been inhabited for thousands of years and evidence for this can be seen in the wonderful Roman wall, much of which remains intact today. Every historical period since the Roman Conquest has left its own mark. There is the oldest castle gatehouse in England at Rougemont Castle, built by William the Conqueror; awe-inspiring Norman towers at Exeter's beautiful Cathedral; picturesque black and white Tudor buildings leaning at impossible angles; Georgian townhouses belonging to woollen cloth merchants from a time often known as Exeter's 'Golden Age' and huge Victorian edifices testifying to the city's wealth and importance.

Because of Exeter's long and bloody history of warfare, rebellion, grisly executions, murder, suicide and disasters (to name but a few horrible events) there is a great deal of ghostly activity in the city for a researcher to uncover. There are also a lot of people who have had paranormal experiences and are more than willing to assist in this research. As I discovered, Exeter is a wonderful place for a ghost hunter to write about!

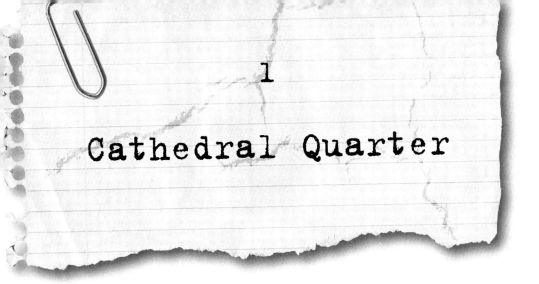

1

Cathedral Quarter

THE Cathedral Quarter is Exeter's most haunted area. Perhaps this isn't surprising as some of the city's oldest buildings are located here, including the magnificent Cathedral itself, sections of the Roman wall and the buried remains of the Roman fort. Many of the buildings surrounding the Cathedral are over 500 years old; it is an area made for ghost hunting!

The Cathedral

Evidence of Christian worship near the Cathedral site goes back to the 400s. The Cathedral structure was finished in 1342, but there have been many additions to this fascinating and beautiful building over the years. As you will see from the following stories, there are spooks-a-plenty!

In 1283, Walter Lechlade, a cathedral choir-leader was murdered in the early morning on his way to his lodgings. Lechlade was known to be unpleasant to his underlings and blatantly dishonest. He had obtained his position undeservedly, because he was a favourite of the Bishop. He was not a popular man and unsurprisingly, he had many enemies.

The ghost of a man dressed in clerical robes is a regular visitor to the cathedral. He goes into the top vestry but when anyone follows him in he is nowhere to be seen even though there is only one doorway. It is said that he is the ghost of Walter Lechlade.

When Parliamentarian forces defeated the Royalists during the English Civil War (1642-49) they undertook a lot of very unpopular changes. Believing that highly decorated church interiors were too close to Catholicism, and that religious buildings should be simple, they painted over the richly coloured and gilded statues in the Cathedral.

When the last statue in Exeter Cathedral's Nuns' Gallery had finally been whitewashed, the painters took down their ladders and began to pack up. One of them happened to glance up into the gallery and was surprised to find that the whitewash had disappeared from one of the statues and that the original gilt could clearly be seen. Thinking they had overlooked one, the statue was repainted. The next morning, though the Cathedral had been locked, the statue's whitewash had disappeared again. The same thing happened over several days.

Exeter Cathedral's South Tower.

The atmospheric Exeter Cathedral, home to spectral monks.

Finally, the senior painter decided to keep watch at night to see what was happening.

As soon as everyone else had left, to his horror the painter saw a pair of disembodied hands begin to clean up the statue with a cloth. The man hurriedly left the Cathedral, never to enter it again. To this day the statue is the only one which is still gilt.

When Parliamentarian Roundhead-soldiers raided the Cathedral to take away items they considered too ornate they were stopped in their tracks when ghostly singing and organ music began suddenly. No choir was present and the organ was playing by itself. Most of the soldiers were God-fearing and had been displeased at being ordered to desecrate the Cathedral in spite of their differing religious beliefs. Many refused to continue. When a group of less principled labourers were found, they finished the work and the organ remained silent.

In the late nineteenth century, derelict buildings near the Cathedral's South Tower were demolished. One night cries of 'help' and 'murder' were heard coming from the rubble of a house which had been knocked down. Alarmed, several locals went to investigate, but found nothing. However, the cries continued for a number of nights. To allay public concern, the Bishop instigated a thorough examination of the location by day. Still nothing was found, but prayers were said at the site. According to a report in Exeter's *Flying Post* dated 14 September 1909, after the prayer reading there were no more disturbing night-time cries.

Several of the Cathedral staff have seen ghostly monks silently chanting in the cloisters. One told me that he only ever sees them for a few seconds before the monks gradually fade away. However, another staff member had the shock of her life when the monk's choir master suddenly turned round and pointed at her irritably as though reprimanding her for interrupting their practice. As you can imagine, the lady left as quickly as she could! A few days later the same lady saw the monks again silently making their way, heads bowed, to the cloisters. Steeling herself, the lady followed them but they had already gone by the time she got to their practise area.

Though both employees were happy for me to use their stories, they asked not to be named as they were worried about upsetting colleagues' religious sensibilities. This is an important point to bear in mind if anyone wishes to conduct their own research.

One of the Cathedral's guides told me that on a number of occasions a strange purple light has been seen moving rapidly around the Lady Chapel. Some people smell a cloying odour like rotting vegetation at the same time. No one has been able to give an explanation for this.

The ghost of a very short nun frequents the nave. Often a strong smell of rosewater, the only perfume nuns are allowed to use, accompanies her manifestation. In a religious building, of course, a nun receives little attention – at first. But when she walks through the wall people do take notice. The spectral sister seems to enjoy avoiding doors.

A tiny nun has been seen to disappear through the north wall of the cathedral, though she is never seen emerging outside. Over the centuries there have been many alterations to the cathedral's structure; so perhaps the nun is actually using doorways which were there during her lifetime but have long since been removed.

A cathedral verger who, it is believed, died in the early 1900s has been seen a number of times fussily stacking hymn books and dusting pews. He is remembered for the fact that his finicky ways made him unpopular with his colleagues.

The figure of a man in overalls sweeping the floor is a usual sight in any building open to the public. What is unusual about this sighting in Exeter Cathedral is that the man has an ethereal appearance and seems to sweep the same part of floor over and over again. A caretaker who has been dead for a number of years was known for thoroughness. He loved the cathedral so much that he often spent his days off there.

Cathedral Green

This lovely area of grass with the picturesque Cathedral as a backdrop is a favourite lunch-time spot for visitors and workers from local businesses. But few realise how close they are to the dead!

Many Christian burials took place on Cathedral Green, the area adjacent to the Cathedral, since the early 500s. Like most areas of the country, Exeter succumbed to the plague numerous times from the 1300s onwards. Many thousands died and were buried on Cathedral Green. By the 1630s there had been so many interments that bodies were stacked several deep and there was no more room. Bishop Hall complained that bits of skeletons sometimes stuck out of the ground. When bones did resurface they were removed to a charnel house which was located near the Cathedral's West Front. Even today, small bits of skeleton lurk under the surface!

In the summer of 1989 a student fell asleep on Cathedral Green. Suddenly he became aware that he was looking down on a building with two wooden spires. The area surrounding it was very rough. The student told the *Exeter Herald*, 'I was then back on earth with a searing pain across my ribcage.'

A toothless, dirty man in ragged old clothing was prodding him violently in the abdomen with a shovel, saying, 'This 'un baint dead'. The student woke up believing it to be a dream and rushed home, feeling somewhat disconcerted, only to find that he was injured. 'Across my chest there was a red wheal which took days to heal,' he said. The student went to see his doctor who described the marks as being similar to burns.

Before 1640 the Cathedral had wooden spires and due to all the burials, the ground on Cathedral Green was very rough. Had the sleeping student been visited by the ghost of an ancient gravedigger disposing of plague victims?

The ghostly apparition of a nun in a deep hood has been seen on Cathedral Green on many occasions. Strangely though, she only seems to appear in July. In the 1940s men stealing lead from a nearby roof attracted the nun's attention one night. She attracted a passer-by to the crime by pointing at the thieves. The men absconded, never to be seen again. Bags containing their spoils were later retrieved from the roof. A number of people have reported that they have seen the nun and have suffered no ill-effects; however, others have died soon after. It is widely believed anyone who does catch sight of her is best advised to hurry away as quickly as possible because if she points at you, your days are numbered!

In the early 1800s the daughter of an Exeter merchant committed suicide. At the time, burial in consecrated ground was not allowed for suicides, and understandably, this troubled her religious father. More importantly, it also seems to have upset the spirit of his daughter.

After the first fall of snow each winter, it is advisable to avoid Cathedral Green at night. Anyone foolhardy enough to go there may see a ghostly hearse pulled by

*Map of Cathedral Green
from the 1590s showing
the probable location of
the charnel house (circled).
(Copyright Exeter Cathedral
Library)*

The Cathedral Green today, but what lies beneath?

four black horses carrying the body of the merchant's daughter. No tracks are left in the snow, either from the wheels or the horse's hooves. Riding in the coach is a pale lady with piercing eyes dressed in white. It is said that anyone who sees the coach will die soon after.

'The Death Coach' a poem about the apparition was written in the 1800s about Lady Howard of Devon:

Now pray step in! My lady saith
Now pray step in and ride
I thank thee, I had rather walk
Than gather to thy side
The wheels go round without a sound
Or tramp of horse's hooves
As cloud at night, in pale moonlight
Along the carriage steals.
I'd rather walk a hundred miles
And run by night and day
Than have that carriage halt for me
And hear my Lady say
Now pray step in and make no din
Step in with me to ride
There's room, I trow, by me for you
And all the world besides.

Cathedral Green has a ghost known as the 'Guardian'. The Cathedral was bombed during the Blitz of 3-4 May 1942. Some of the ancient stained glass windows were destroyed and the fourteenth-century Chapel of St James was badly damaged.

Firemen, wardens and other volunteers rushed to the scene to try and save as much of the structure as possible. Hardly noticed in the confusion, a strange pale-faced man with deep-set red eyes and long dark clothes stood on Cathedral Green observing the scene. Later, a fireman recalled seeing the figure pointing to the sky, and shaking its head. The fireman turned back to his task but when he looked round again a few seconds later the figure had disappeared.

In the 1990s two workmen were knocking down an unstable part of the low wall surrounding Cathedral Green prior to rebuilding it. They were puzzled to see an odd looking 'tramp' with reddened eyes watching their work. He silently raised his arm and pointed at the dismantled wall. When the workmen looked again a few seconds later he was gone. They looked along the long pavement in both directions but he had disappeared.

Cathedral Close and Cathedral Yard

The wonderful buildings on Cathedral Close and Cathedral Yard form right-angled boundaries along two sides of the cathedral perimeter. Steeped in history, almost all the buildings have spooky stories to tell.

Ask Restaurant
This building was once used to accommodate clergymen. In 1730 it was converted into a townhouse and its present façade was constructed.

The most famous haunted story associated with Ask is that of John, a young monk, and Martha, a young nun from the 1600s. At this time, the cellar of the building was used as a morgue and John had the job of laying out bodies. Martha used to visit him in secret and they fell in love. Eventually, Martha discovered that she was expecting a child. The disgrace was too much for the unfortunate couple to bear and they committed suicide by throwing themselves down the well in the building's courtyard. Many years later when the well was excavated, two skeletons were discovered. These are now on display

The entrance to Ask Restaurant, where you'll dine with ghosts.

in the Well House Pub's basement (*see* the Well House story).

Since then there have been an abundance of haunted happenings. Hazy figures in flowing black robes, described by one of the staff as 'religious', have been seen flitting around the courtyard. Sudden icy drafts regularly occur, in winter and summer alike, in places where there is no flow of air. When going through the building's entrance, superstitious people used to say 'hello' to John and Martha in the hope that it would ward off any evil spirits.

Before becoming a restaurant, Ask was a working men's club for many years. On several occasions ghostly figures were seen on the security cameras and to the horror of the doorman, tin storage boxes would regularly move by themselves, sometimes violently crashing to the floor.

A man was once doing some decorating work at Ask during the night so as not to disrupt day-time business. He reported seeing a strange figure dressed in white. The man was a little shaken, but continued with his work. Later he tried to enter the bathroom, but found its door locked even though there could have been no one in it. Suddenly the door crashed open; the man fled.

The cleaners have nicknamed one of the resident ghosts 'Ethel'. One evening, in a playful attempt to summon the apparition, one of the cleaners spelt out its name aloud. There was no response. When another cleaning lady tried she mistakenly spelled out 'Eleth'. There was an immediate excited rustling sound. This happened each time the name was misspelled. The cleaning ladies began to have doubts as to the ghost's sex because its mischievous behaviour in emptying bins all over the floor and switching the vacuum cleaner to 'blow' were not the habits any female would adopt! Perhaps the ghost was indeed a man with the unusual name 'Eleth'.

Bishop of Crediton's House

In 1050 the bishop's seat was moved from the nearby town of Crediton to Exeter as the city is walled and well protected. In 1550 the Bishop of Crediton's accommodation was constructed and it is still used for this purpose. The building features an arched oak and metal door which opens onto a courtyard garden.

The niece of a recent Bishop was startled to see three men in Elizabethan costume in the courtyard. When she screamed, the Bishop's wife rushed out, only to see the men vanish through the wall before her eyes. The Bishop's pet dog was known as a very friendly and calm creature that never barked or growled. Except, that is, when he was taken past this wall – then he would howl and snarl, shaking in terror.

The door leading to the Bishop of Creditor's courtyard.

It is said that the nursery rhyme 'Hickory Dickory Dock' was about a white cat which once ran hissing loudly through the cathedral and chased a mouse into the famous fifteenth-century Astronomical Clock during a service many years ago. The clock mechanism made a loud noise and proceedings were disrupted while the cat was removed.

In modern times the shape of a one eyed ghostly-white cat has been seen running from the Cathedral's north tower and across the green. Hissing as it goes; it startles passers-by before disappearing through the medieval cat flap in the building next to the Bishop of Crediton's house. Is this the same disruptive feline still up to mischief?

The Devon and Exeter Institution

The building was once a family house, but has been a private library since 1813. The impressive interior combines ornate Georgian decor with comfortable old-fashioned armchairs, sumptuous rugs and high shelves full of wonderful old books. Modern visitors are left with the impression that they have actually stepped back to a more elegant time. I had heard about the extent of ghostly activity before I visited the building and if ever a place looked and felt haunted, this is it.

The late Theo Brown, a well-known local author and paranormal expert, once spent many months carrying out research for her book *The Fate of the Dead*, in the library. After giving a talk on the subject to fellow Institution members, one asked her the name of the old lady wearing a large cross who always accompanied the writer while she was researching. The old lady was often seen reading over the writer's shoulder sadly shaking her head. Theo was adamant that she always did her research alone, and that she would never consider bringing anyone else to the library without permission.

After a book publicity party, given by the author at the Institution, she took the guests on a tour of Cathedral Green. One person, a wheelchair user, remained alone in the Institution and was horrified when a strange wind inside the library blew many books off the shelves, damaging some beyond repair. Oddly, only the books consulted by the writer were dislodged. Was the old lady who accompanied the writer a religious ghost who disagreed with the subject matter?

In the 1980s the caretaker, Mrs Andrews, reported seeing a man dressed in nineteenth-century naval officer's clothing. The caretaker recognised the sailor as one whose picture appeared in a book of uniforms. As she looked on in astonishment, the sailor picked the very book off the shelf and began to read it. As quickly as he appeared, the book and sailor simply disappeared.

The haunted bookshelves in the Devon and Exeter Institution.

The Devon and Exeter Institution's inner doorway.

Mrs Andrews' dog refused to go anywhere near the shelves containing naval books, though it would happily go to sleep anywhere else in the building. Perhaps Mrs Andrews' most frightening experience happened when she was showing a group of visitors around the library. At the time, renovations were taking place and there was plastic sheeting on the floor. Standing near the spot where the naval man had been seen, Mrs Andrews was relating the story. Suddenly the plastic sheet in front of her wrinkled up and rustled as if someone was walking on it.

When renovations were completed Mrs Andrews polished the floor in the entrance hall, which had been badly scratched during the work. Late one night, when everyone else had left the building, she poured a liquid sealer onto the floor to protect it before retiring to her own accommodation at the back of the building. The next morning when she went to check if the floor was dry there were footprints from a little child's shoes all over the sealer.

On a number of occasions, when in her rooms, Mrs Andrews reported seeing the ghost of a little girl in 1950s style school uniform. When other staff members expressed concern she replied, 'Oh it's nothing to worry about. She doesn't frighten me. I feel sorry for her, she seems lost'.

Staff have grown used to a carefully locked door opening of its own accord and lights switching themselves on and off, but the unpleasant smells, like overused cheap perfume, which sometimes permeate the air are more disconcerting.

Recently a library assistant was looking for a book which had been put back in the wrong place when there was a sudden bang behind her. As she turned round she caught sight of a shadowy figure hurrying away.

On the floor at her feet the assistant found the missing book.

Roger Brien has been Chief Librarian at the Devon and Exeter Institution for over twenty years. He was happy to talk to me about the haunted building. Roger told me that he had worked with many trustworthy colleagues who were receptive to the Institution's ghosts, but had only had one ghostly experience himself. One evening when no one else was in the library he saw a dark figure flit across the open doorway which separates the inner and outer libraries. When he mentioned this to a colleague the next day he was told that she and other staff members had seen a strange cloaked figure in exactly the same place. Roger himself is level-headed and most definitely not given to flights of fancy.

Mol's Coffee Shop

This striking timber-framed sixteenth-century building is on the corner of Cathedral close. In the Tudor period, Mol's was a meeting place for Exeter's fine gentlemen, but it was never a coffee shop – the beverage had not appeared in England at this time! It is said that Sir Francis Drake planned tactics for the defeat of the Spanish Armada while at Mol's during the very hot spring of 1588. Locals were startled on several occasions to hear Drake's excited shouting and the barking of his friend's dog through the open windows of the first floor as he enacted his battle plan.

Today the building houses 'The Collection', a luxury shoe and leather goods store which opened there in 2009. The owner told me that on the first floor, which is the storeroom for large leather bags and suitcases, he often finds windows open when he has locked them shut. The barking of a dog can sometimes be heard in the upstairs storage room, though there is no dog in the shop or in any of the nearby premises.

The storeroom of
'The Collection' housed in Mol's Coffee House.

The 'Tea on the Green' Restaurant.

Numbers 8, 9 and 9a

This red sandstone and timber structure was originally built as three houses around 1450. For many years the large medieval hall has housed a law library and solicitor's practice.

Hayley used to work in the building as a secretary and recalls being told that the basement was haunted by a trapped spirit called Emily. She was initially very sceptical about this tale. Then another secretary, known for her unflappable nature, had to visit the basement to retrieve some old files. While there she heard someone say her name, though no one else was in the room. She then heard a girl sobbing and felt a cold wind around her face. She was so frightened she would not go back down to the basement again and left her job shortly afterwards.

A figure with a misshaped head and a severe limp wearing clothing from the Victorian period has also been seen moving across Cathedral Green and walking up and down outside this building as if waiting for someone.

Tea on the Green

The ghost of a beautiful woman, naked to the waist, has been seen in this restaurant. It is thought that she was the daughter of one of Exeter's mayors from the 1500s. He was ruthlessly ambitious and sent his daughter to the building, which at the time was the home of a cathedral priest. He hoped that the priest would be unable to resist her beauty and thus be open to blackmail. Though some clerics were known for their unpriestly behaviour in those days, it was not a good idea for such antics to reach the ear of the bishop! The hapless young lady was never seen again and the priest denied having entertained her. In the 1980s when work was being done by the water board on Cathedral Green, the skeleton of a woman was discovered. Locals believe that this was the missing young lady.

The last known sighting of the lady with no top was in 1996 when the café was known as Hanson's. The waitress who saw it now works in a café in another area of the city. She told me that she was initially annoyed at the appearance of the topless lady, thinking it was a silly student prank. When the lady disappeared through the wall the waitress ran out of the café and has never returned. Until then she had put up with things going missing and turning up in odd places, or piles of plates left safely in the sink suddenly crashing to the floor. The semi-clad ghost was the final straw.

Cathedral Yard

The Abbot's Lodge

This chilling story was recounted in the *Exeter Gazette* of 8 November 1919. For many years the Lodge was the townhouse of the Abbot of Tavistock, but by the early 1900s it had become a private house. One night, the owner had visitors including two men and a family with two young daughters. The girls were in bed when they heard loud scuffling and banging outside their bedroom door, as if men were fighting. This was followed by something bumping down the stairs. Next morning the girls asked what had happened. Surprised, the men said that they had not come out of their room all night. The owner of the house then told a story. One of the abbots who had occupied the house was murdered in an upstairs room. His assailants put his body in a sack and dragged it down the stairs. The previous night had been the anniversary of the murder and the girls had heard it in ghostly re-enactment.

The lodge was destroyed in the bombing of May 1942, but when the bombsite was later cleared ghostly bumping and screams were heard by the startled workmen.

The Globe Hotel

The Globe Hotel was Tudor in origin but had been extended and altered during the Georgian era. The hotel was burned down during the Blitz in 1942.

A resident ghost here was fond of Americans – particularly senior military figures who often stayed during the war. Although never seen, her footsteps and rustling dress could be heard, and whenever the guests included American soldiers a strong smell of perfume could be detected.

Pizza Express

This beautiful sixteenth-century building commands a wonderful view of the cathedral. From the 1840s it became the Cathedral Café, eventually becoming the famous Mrs Tinley's Teashop in the 1930s. In 1996 the present occupants, Pizza Express, took the building over. When I visited, the recently appointed manager was very helpful. He had heard about the haunted goings-on in his restaurant and was happy to show me around and let me speak to the staff.

One such sighting took place long before they moved in. In the winter of 1982 the ghostly outlines of four monks were seen warming themselves around a fireplace which had not been in use for many years.

A more recent pest comes in the shape of 'Percy Poltergeist', as the staff have named him. He makes mischief by fiddling with the controls of the music system. A waiter told me that he has had to replace the plug on the stereo several times because Percy has yanked it out of the wall. I asked if, perhaps, it was simply a colleague playing

The Pizza Express fireplace.

tricks. The waiter replied, 'No, it happens when no one else is near. And anyway, no one would want to damage the equipment.' Percy, it seems, has no such qualms!

Pizza Express have recently refurbished the building and a glass wall panel now commemorates another resident ghost. This one, a man in 'ancient costume', has been seen by restaurant customers over the years sitting at their table while they eat. After listening to the conversation for a while, he calmly gets up and walks off down the steps to the cellar.

During my visit I went down to the cellar myself. Although brightly decorated and well lit, there was a very unpleasant atmosphere, which intensified as I descended the steps. I was very glad to get out and can well understand why most of the staff don't like being down there alone.

Pizza Express Flat

Dave, the owner of the flat above the restaurant, has had a number of strange experiences there which point to poltergeist activity. Bulbs go missing from the ceiling lights and lamps. Items of clothing disappear from their usual shelf, only to turn up in places where Dave would never put them. Scarily, a heavy bookshelf fell over although it was firmly sited and would have needed great force to shift it. If Dave had been nearer when it happened he would have been seriously hurt. In the kitchen a knife which was resting securely on the worktop, suddenly flew across the room and landed on the floor. Recently, out of the corner of his eye Dave saw his rucksack move. It rose to about a metre from the floor before falling as if someone had dropped it. Often, the temperature in the flat changes suddenly, even on warm sunny days. At times it becomes so cold in the kitchen that Dave can see his breath as if it was winter.

In 1283 a city guard who lived in accommodation on the site of Pizza Express was among those executed for the murder of Walter Lechlade, Bishop Quinel's very unpopular assistant. The guard claimed to have fallen asleep at his post, but was accused of complicity in the murder.

The Royal Clarence Hotel

The Royal Clarence Hotel was built in 1769 and is reputedly the first inn in England to use the term 'hotel'. The word 'Royal' was added to the building's name after the Duke and Duchess of Clarence (later King William IV and Queen Adelaide) stayed there in the 1820s.

One of the bedrooms is actually haunted by the Duchess of Clarence. Julian Wilkinson, the hotel manager, told me that porters have seen her pale anxious ghost, complete with early nineteenth-century head-dress, looking out of the room's bay window apparently waiting for the return of her notoriously unfaithful husband (who had a number of amorous adventures during his stay in the city).

Julian told me that the fourth floor rooms were once used as staff living quarters. Today they have been converted into very luxurious guest bedrooms. Despite their comfortable surroundings, however, some guests have had their nights interrupted by the brief but horrifying image of a screaming woman with her hair on fire.

In 2006, a young girl in a maid's uniform was seen struggling up the stairs in tears

The Royal Clarence Hotel.

with a large bucket of coal. The first instinct of the guest who saw her was to help her with her load but the girl shook her head at his offer and continued on her way. When the man reached the top of the stairs seconds later, the girl had vanished. On making enquiries he was told that there are no coal fires in the hotel and there haven't been since the 1930s.

A faint ghostly man in an old-fashioned night shirt has been seen walking around late at night by one of hotel the porters.

Recently my friend Alice stayed at the Royal Clarence Hotel, during a visit to the city. Alice is not a nervous person; indeed, she is very sceptical about ghost stories and had not heard any about the hotel before her visit. After a pleasant evening, which she assures me only included two alcoholic drinks, Alice went to bed. Her room overlooked St Martin's Lane and the Ship Inn. A while later she was woken by a rumbling noise outside her window. Thinking that staff were moving metal barrels and cross because it was so late, Alice looked out. Trundling along St Martins Lane was a horse and cart with metal-clad wheels driven by a man in an old-fashioned cloak and an eighteenth-century three-cornered hat.

The next day Alice was told some of Royal Clarence's ghost stories. 'But after what I saw I'd already lost some of my scepticism,' she told me.

The site of the Royal Clarence hotel was once the location of a townhouse belonging to the family of Walter Raleigh. A sea captain of his acquaintance visited Raleigh, who was surprised to find his friend looking very ill. The man explained that he was being haunted by the ghost of a very unpleasant man who had lost a lot of money he had invested in one of the captain's trading expeditions.

Raleigh and his friend sat either side of the parlour fire discussing what to do about the problem. To help him think, Raleigh filled his pipe with tobacco, which was a new craze in Europe at the time. They were somewhat surprised to hear the sound of coughing coming from across the room, accompanied by loud tut-tutting. As they looked round, the faint shape of the disgruntled investor could be seen waving as if to dispel the tobacco smoke. Startled, Raleigh and his friend stood up to leave, but before they could move the ghost shook his fist and disappeared through the closed window, never to be seen again.

The Well House Pub

The Well House is part of the Royal Clarence Hotel and is built on Roman foundations. In the cellar is a Roman well from which the pub takes its name. The cellar, particularly, is known locally for its ghostly stories.

A human skeleton is displayed in a glass case in the gloomy cellar of the Well House; it was found buried outside Ask Restaurant many years ago. Research done in 2002 suggests that the skeleton is a mix of male and female bones. Could it be the remains of tragic John and Martha? (*see* the Ask Restaurant story).

In the late eighteenth century, a young man by the name of Richard Bratstone frequently enjoyed boozy evenings at the Well House. One night, after numerous drinks, his friends set him a challenge. If he spent the night locked securely in the pub cellar, alone, without any light, they would give him two 2s. The cellar was rumoured to be haunted by an evil spirit which went by the name of Lucy, but Richard, who was short of money after his evening's drinking, agreed to the bet. His friends intended to let him out before daylight, but they carried on drinking at another pub and forgot all about him. The next morning, when they opened the cellar door, his friends were puzzled to find that Richard had disappeared. They then noticed a wizened old man in the corner and asked him if he had seen their friend. The old man, who was obviously very ill, could only gasp and gesture weakly towards the Roman well. At this point one of the young men realised that the sickly figure was wearing Richard's clothes. They hurriedly carried the figure outside into the light, where they recognised him as their friend. Richard gasped once more and died with a look of absolute terror on his face. What dreadful experience had befallen Richard in that dark cellar?

One of the barmen, Paul, told me that in the ground-floor bar bottles regularly fall off shelves for no apparent reason. At the end of each evening the shelves are restocked neatly. Often the next day the shelves are found in disarray with bottles, bags of snacks and towels strewn all over the floor. The manager is certain that no one has access to the bar once it is closed.

While in the bar Paul has also heard strange groaning and rasping sounds from the cellar. Such is the fright among the staff that none of them are willing to spend time alone in the cellar, which is used for storage. At one time or another they have all experienced the evil atmosphere which pervades it.

In September 2010 I conducted an investigation in the Well House cellar accompanied by paranormal investigator Tony Eccles, author of *A Different Sky*, as well as sound-engineer Lee Rawlings and my partner Seal Faulkner (who refused to believe in ghosts). At closing time we descended into the cellar which, though well lit, has a strangely heavy atmosphere, not helped of course by the glass case con-

taining the skeleton at one end! Exploring the chamber, we discovered a definite cold spot near the ancient well (which is at the other end of the cellar from the skeleton). We sat and kept watch for quite a while, but saw nothing out of the ordinary. Before leaving the empty pub we set up Lee's recording equipment, which I retrieved the next day.

The recorder had switched itself off after only one and a half hours though the batteries were new and should have lasted for at least six hours. Lee checked the equipment out and nothing was wrong with it. I was rather disappointed until Lee told me that this sometimes happens when there is poltergeist activity.

Listening to the recording was uninspiring at first, as nothing much could be made out. Then we distinctly heard a gasping breath followed by what sounded like something wooden hitting the floor. A little later on, a sound like dripping water could be heard. The cellar is dry and I wondered if the noise could have come from water pipes, but there are none in the old part of the cellar, which has solid stone walls. For quite a while there was nothing of interest on the CD, and then we heard the sound of breathing again followed by what can only be described as a sound of exclamation which made my hair stand on end. This noise came just before the recording stopped.

I returned to the Well House, where I was assured that no one had been near the recording equipment once it was left there.

Other Cathedral Quarter Areas

Bedford House, Bedford Street
Today Bedford Street is part of the new Princesshay Shopping Centre and

The mysterious skeleton in the Well House Pub.

The Well House basement showing the Roman well and behind it, the wall where the hovering light appeared.

Princess Henrietta Anne. (Copyright Exeter City Council)

there are no old buildings left because of war-time bombing. However, from the 1530s until its destruction in the Blitz, Bedford House, on Bedford Square, was the most impressive residence in Exeter.

Henrietta Anne, the ninth child of King Charles I and sister of the future Charles II, was born at Bedford House on 16 June 1644 during the English Civil War. She was smuggled to France before the Parliamentarian forces defeated her father; Henrietta Ann eventually married the violent and insanely jealous Duke of Orléans. The only person at the French court who dared to offer her friendship was Sir Jeffery Hudson, who was a dwarf. The Princess died aged twenty-six. It was rumoured hat she had been murdered by her husband.

In the 1930s a Mrs Cornish visited Bedford House which, by then, had become a museum. A strange queasy feeling overcame the lady and the curator brought an old chair for her to sit on. As she looked out of the window, Mrs Cornish saw a strange and sad sight – a frail young woman in old-fashioned clothes was limping sorrowfully along.

Many people since then have reported seeing two apparitions in the area – a young woman dressed in ornate seventeenth-century style and a small man who holds the woman's hand. Are these the ghosts of unhappy Henrietta Anne and her loyal friend Jeffery? The two mysterious figures were seen as recently as 2005 when construction of the new shopping area began.

Gemstar Jewellers 1-2 Catherine Street
This pair of three-storey buildings dates from the 1450s and is located on the corner of Catherine Street and St Martin's Lane next to the Ship Inn.

Originally the buildings were used as Annuellars accommodation. Annuellars were priests who said Mass on the anniversary of a person's death. They were well paid for the job and it is said that after midnight you can still the noise hear their ghostly carousing coming from the jewellers.

St Catherine's Almshouses, Catherine Street
The atmospheric red sandstone ruins of St Catherine's Almshouses are located on Catherine Street, just off Cathedral Green. Built in 1457, they housed some of Exeter's destitute and infirm for many years. In 1685 a group of Irish Baptists who had escaped persecution in their homeland were allowed to stay at the almshouses.

Falling victim to the bombing in 1942, the almshouses are now derelict and roofless. In spite of this, strange music and laughter have been heard coming from the building late at night. Locals believe that the ghosts of the Irish Baptists are still celebrating finding their new safe home.

St Catherine's Almshouses.

Milkmaid Café, Catherine Street

The café is a modern building and stands next to the ruins of St Catherine's Almshouses. Though the current manager has never experienced anything strange, a former waitress, Joan, reported seeing a man in a long brown coat in the ground floor café late one evening in 2000. Thinking that one of the customers had somehow been locked in, she hurried to let him out. As she passed the man, Joan caught a glimpse of a cross hanging around the man's neck. Opening the door, she turned to apologise. The man had disappeared.

The National Institute of Medical Herbalists, Palace Gate

During renovations a builder was working alone when suddenly a dreadful smell like rotting flesh pervaded the air. He felt an inexplicable sense of foreboding, and though it was a hot day became very chilled. The builder left hurriedly on his first day and refused to go back in. Another workman was employed and managed to stay for a week before telling the proprietor that he was leaving for good. The workman complained that he heard heavy breathing behind him although he was alone in the building and that a bag containing spare clothes was ransacked and its contents spread about the room. The final straw came when, returning to the locked building after lunch, he found his tools thrown into a corner with their blades damaged.

The Ship Inn, St Martin's Lane

The Ship Inn was the favourite hostelry of Sir Francis Drake, famous for defeating the Spanish Armada. It is an atmospheric old

The Ship Inn.

building with original beams, sloping floors and the tiny window panes associated with the Elizabethan era. Unsurprisingly, there are several spooky tales attached to the place and the manager, Mark, who believes that there at least five ghosts in his pub, was happy to share the stories with me.

A ghostly man in richly coloured Elizabethan costume has been seen lurking in the pub's corners. Over recent years, after he has been seen, staff have complained that items have gone missing. They later turn up in unlikely places.

In the restaurant on the first floor the ghost of a lady in a dark dress and an Elizabethan ruff has been seen on several occasions. Late at night the manager, in his accommodation above, has heard loud noises and crashing coming from the restaurant. On investigating he has found tables and chairs overturned and cutlery strewn across the floor. Since having the restaurant floor carpeted in 2007, Mark has not been disturbed, but now finds napkins and menus thrown about. One of the tables in the bar has a clear view up the stairs to the restaurant. A number of customers have seen a lady in old-fashioned clothing climbing the stairs.

In the Victorian period the landlord of the Ship Inn had a disabled son. He was deaf, had fits and was unable to walk. Like many disabled people in those days, the unfortunate boy was hidden away, living most of his life in the attic. When he grew older, however, he occasionally escaped. A story went around the town that he was responsible for the murder of two prostitutes, though this seems never to have been proven. Today, none of the staff like going into the attic as there is a very creepy atmosphere. A barman reported hearing cackling and whimpering up there as if someone was trying to speak, but couldn't. Then he was grabbed by unseen hands and pushed, almost falling down the stairs. The barman left his job soon after.

Mark has been woken up several times during the night to see a little girl in a long dress lying on his bed trying to cuddle him. 'She's just a child and seems really sweet. She doesn't bother me at all,' Mark told me.

He has also seen her playing in the corridor outside his room before disappearing through the wall where there was once a door. The corridor is used to store extra drinks and food at Christmas. In 2009 one of the barmen was stacking boxes there when he noticed the little girl sitting on the stairs.

The cleaner told Mark that while cleaning the front windows alone in the building, he saw tiny handprints appear on the inside of the cleaned glass as if a little child was touching it.

In 2009 the building was visited by Elizabeth, a medium, and the spirit of a little girl told her that she was called Polly. Elizabeth told me that Mark was right to be unafraid of Polly. 'She was the granddaughter of a cook who lived at the Ship before the First World War,' Elizabeth told me. 'She was very fond of her grandfather and used to stay with him in the room Mark now occupies.'

A very tall ghost in a cloak has been seen in various parts of the building. Elizabeth claimed, 'He was the owner of the Ship in the mid-Victorian era and was named Peters. And even though he knows his presence sometimes worries people, he can't help continuing to take an interest in the place!'

One night, when Mark was working alone in the office, something made him turn round in his chair. The Victorian ghost was leaning over his shoulder examining the business accounts. I can't help wondering how the nosy spook copes with decimal currency and metric measures!

During particularly busy times staff have reported being clapped on the back in a friendly manner, though no one is there. Peters' ghost carries a large ring of keys and is often heard rattling them before he is seen.

I asked Mark what his staff thought of all the ghostly activity. 'New staff are usually quite unnerved when they first see something strange', he told me. 'But eventually they get used to it. Only two have left because they were too scared. Mind you, most of the staff don't like being on any of the floors alone and they can't understand how I can stay here at night!'

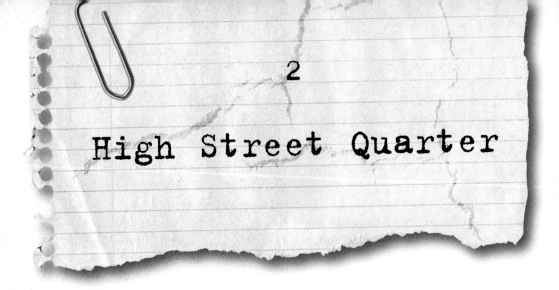

High Street Quarter

TODAY the High Street Quarter is a fascinating mix of the old and the new. Large stores rub shoulders with quirky individual shops in quaintly ancient alleys and tiny old churches hide amidst the modern architecture. There are buildings from every period from the Tudors to the twenty-first century and tales of horrendous fires, plague and suicide abound, each with an accompanying ghost story!

Bella Italia, Queen Street

In the 1850s the building was known as the Queens Hotel. Today it is occupied by a branch of Bella Italia Restaurants.

In the 1970s, a young man and his friends who had formed a band used to practice in the cellars. One night strange and unexplained things began to happen. The room suddenly went very cold, glasses began to move on their own, and the drummer's sticks, which had been left on the drum, began to bang though no one was holding them. The young men told the owner of the building, who said that she would never go into the cellar herself. Her staff continually complained that every time they tidied the cellar it was messy again soon after, even though no one had been in. A bar-maid left because she kept seeing the ghost of a Victorian woman in the kitchen and a plumber fitting some pipe work claimed to have seen his tool box move up and down on its own.

Coolings Wine Bar and Restaurant, Gandy Street

Gandy Street is a very old area of the city. In Coolings cellars, ghostly activity has been known to take place quite regularly. Valves on beer kegs are turned off when no one is there and when a staff member goes to investigate, the cellar lights turn on and off. In the restaurant, menus often fall off tables when no one is near enough to dislodge them. When I talked to the manager he had only worked there for a few weeks and had not experienced any ghostly activity, but he told me that a former member of staff who was now retired had heard a strange whispering voice in the restaurant.

Gandy Street Plague Victims

Gandy Street was once the area of the city where leather craftsmen worked. The street was destitute and filthy; the discarded food waste encouraged black rats. Fleas on the rats carried the plague virus. The worst outbreak in Exeter was in 1348. There were so many victims on Gandy Street that the men employed to drive the cart which removed the bodies refused to go there. The dead piled up and the rats became bloated from eating the corpses.

At night a ghost with a blackened, pustule covered face has been seen by passers-by. If anyone is brave enough to approach, the ghost promptly vanishes. Frightened locals in the area organised an exorcism in the 1950s. The ghost has not been seen since, but in the dead of night the wheels of an unseen cart can still be heard rattling over Gandy Street's ancient cobbles.

Northernhay Street
In 1984, a young girl living in Northernhay Street refused to comb her hair, declaring that when she sat at her dressing table she felt she was being watched through the mirror. In an attempt to prove her daughter wrong, her exasperated mother sprayed the mirror with hair spray. She was horrified to see a red eye in the glass which began to spin round like a vortex before slowly disappearing. The *Exeter Weekly News* of 31 August of that year reported that the dressing table was burned and its mirror smashed and buried.

In No. 4 Northernhay Street the tenant observed strange lights on the living-room wall. His cat would run howling across the room away from the lights. Each time it stopped in the same position and immediately calmed down. The man did some research and found that many years before there had been a fire in the room which had been contained by a staircase. Where his cat stopped was the location of the stairs.

Old High School, Musgrave Row
In the early seventeenth century the school's headmaster William Perryman

Gandy Street.

was known for his cruelty to the boys in his charge. It was his belief that boys should be beaten every day. A number of parents complained as their children were too frightened to learn anything and truancy was high. Perryman maintained that his actions were merely to keep order and the matter was dropped. Then a pupil at the school drowned himself because he was so scared of Perryman. This time the town council took the situation seriously and Perryman was sacked. Though the original school building was destroyed in the bombing of 1942, on dark nights it is still possible to hear the cries of the unfortunate schoolboys.

The Phoenix, Bradninch Place
Today, Exeter Phoenix is an arts centre with space for performing arts and visual arts.

In the late nineteenth century the building was used by the University of Exeter, but it had originally been a private hospital. Several years ago new performance spaces were built into the basement. Exeter Archaeology Field Unit were brought in to excavate the site before building work commenced; they unearthed evidence of operating theatres, including channels in the floor down which blood would have flowed during operations.

The building was used as a hospital at a time when medical knowledge was very crude compared to today. There would have been lots of gruesome deaths among the patients. Nowadays the basement is the scene of lively performances by various drama and music groups and there are few strange manifestations during these times.

However, when there are no performances taking place, the basement becomes gloomy and forbidding, in spite of the fact that it is brightly lit. This is when equipment seems to be moved, although no one is around to do this. People have reported hearing strange shuffling noises and faint screams. Are these the ghosts of long-dead patients who met horrible deaths at the former hospital?

Sound technician Lee Rawlings, who has helped with investigations for this book, runs a regular radio show at Phonic FM in the basement of the Phoenix. Several of his colleagues who run late-night shows have seen the figure of a man in strange old fashioned clothing pass the open door of the radio studio before suddenly disappearing in the corridor.

Theatre Royal, Longbrook Street

Before electricity became commonplace fires in theatres were all too common, as they often relied on candle light. In fact, there were three establishments called the Theatre Royal on the same site in Exeter. The first two burned down – and while the first fire caused irreparable damage to the theatre, the second in 1887 was disastrous. It happened during a packed performance and caused the deaths of over 180 people. The tragedy led to vastly improved safety features in all theatres in England (including Exeter's third Theatre Royal, which opened in 1889). To begin with the theatre was a venue for stage productions, but from the early 1900s it began to show films and continued to do so throughout the heyday of cinema before closing in 1962.

In 1961 a young film projectionist, Tony, attended the theatre's staff Christmas party which went on until 2 a.m. Concerned about his girlfriend, who was rather drunk, he and his friend decided that the three of them should stay the night in the staffroom. The two lads laid the young lady on an old sofa and covered her with coats before bedding themselves down on the floor. Not surprisingly, they found it difficult to sleep. After about an hour Tony thought he could hear footsteps in the nearby corridor.

'I knew I had let everyone out before locking up, so I was a bit surprised to hear someone walking about. Then I decided that perhaps some of my pals had come back as a joke,' Tony said.

He and his friend went to investigate, but could see no one. The two young men returned to their makeshift bedroom only to hear more noises in the corridor. 'We were just lads and liked a jape,' Tony told me. 'So we ran out of the room giggling expecting to catch one of the other boys. We were quick enough to see the heavy metal door leading to the backstage area closing. Then we heard lots of running feet'.

Putting the lights on, Tony ran backstage, but again could see no one. Then he realised that the only exit was locked from the inside. By this time the lads were scared and decided to wake the girl up and get her home.

After the Christmas holiday Tony told the tale to the theatre manager. He said that the building was haunted by the spirits of those who had perished in the fire in 1887. A lot of the victims had died in the backstage area while trying to find their way out in the thick smoke.

Today there is a business area where the Theatre Royal once stood. No one in any of the offices seems to have heard or seen anything odd. Perhaps the destruction of the third Theatre Royal allowed the unfortunate spirits to escape from their theatrical tomb.

The Thistle Hotel, Queen Street

The Thistle Hotel, a fine Victorian building, was constructed on the site of an old prison and the gallows were located in the position now occupied by the hotel's flagpole. A tunnel was found during the building of the hotel which may have been a prisoners' escape attempt.

Several guests have reported hearing clanking noises like rattling chains. A lady wearing a ragged, long dress and thought to be one of the condemned prisoners is said to haunt the corridors in the early hours of the morning.

A few months after the Thistle opened, a young female guest gassed herself in her room. She had been jilted and the hotel should have been where she spent her honeymoon. Perhaps the 'grey lady' is, in fact, the ghost of this suicide victim whose spirit has been unable to find rest?

Underground Passages, Paris Street

The Underground Passages were constructed in the medieval period to bring fresh piped water into Exeter from clean springs outside the city wall. The pipe repairers had a terrible job working for hours at a time in dark, wet and cramped conditions. Today I work part-time as a guide in the Underground Passages and thankfully, comfort and safety are much improved for visitors who enjoy guided historical tours.

The atmospheric passages look as though there should be a lot of haunting activity. A visitor who was a medium did once report that he felt the presence of a sad small boy in dirty clothes. This is interesting as little children were once employed as labourers in the passages.

Unfortunately none of the guides have ever seen or felt anything remotely spooky – tales of a Victorian gentleman on a penny farthing bicycle, naughty ghostly nuns meeting their monk boyfriends and marching Roman Soldiers with fierce faces can be put down to over-enthusiastic guides entertaining groups of school children during Halloween half-term!

The Thistle Hotel.

High Street

Sidwell Street, which merges with the High Street, is also included in this section because of its close proximity.

Large parts of the High Street and Sidwell Street were bombed during the Second World War but there are still many wonderful old buildings and many haunted tales.

Clinton Cards

I worked at Clinton's for a few weeks over the Christmas period when I moved to Devon in 2000. One of my first jobs was tidying the attic storeroom with another assistant. I was immediately struck by the creepy atmosphere. Later the manageress, Sandra, told me that the building has a resident ghost – a man in Victorian top hat and long coat. He has been seen in the attic a few times and most of the staff refused to stay there alone for long. More often the manageress saw the ghost in her basement office. Some mornings important documents were found jumbled up and staff have learned to lock them away at the end of the day. Sandra, a practical down-to-earth lady, is not too worried about the ghost. 'I don't think he's an evil spirit,' she told me. 'More curious or mischievous really. And now we lock all the paperwork away he does no harm!'

Co-Operative Bank

St Lawrence's Church, which dated from the thirteenth century, once stood on the site of the Co-Operative Bank. Unfortunately, the church was destroyed during the bombing of May 1942, but a ghostly organ rendition of 'Jerusalem' has been heard at the location. 'Jerusalem' was the organist's favourite piece and he was playing it during the bombing raid.

A plaque commemorating the church can now be seen on the wall of the Co-Operative Bank.

Commemorative plaque on the Co-Operative Bank.

Ernest Jones Jewellers

Staff at Ernest Jones believe that their shop is haunted by the ghost of a seventeenth-century woman who was once a remand prisoner in the adjoining Guildhall basement. The building housing Ernest Jones' dates from the 1500s and has been used for many purposes over the years.

Throughout the 1980s a clothes boutique was located here. In the basement storeroom members of staff frequently saw the ghostly figure of a young woman among the racks of clothes. One day the manager was horrified to see a disembodied head floating towards her before vanishing through a wall. The *Exeter Weekly News* of 17 August 1984 reported the sighting.

'It looked like a young woman. She had a nasty injury to her face and was screaming, but there was no sound,' the manager said. 'I'm not too happy to be down there alone now!'

Despite knowing this story, the Earnest Jones staff members feel that that their spook, nicknamed 'Lulu', is more mischievous than malevolent. Some of her activities can be a nuisance, though.

One day near Christmas 2007 when the shop was particularly busy the jeweller who carries out alterations returned from lunch to find that he couldn't open the door to his basement workroom. He and several of the staff managed to push the door open using their combined weight. Behind it a bench had been wedged. No one else was in the room and the skylight, the only other exit, is barred.

From upstairs the staff have often heard furniture in the basement restroom being moved when no one is there. Only a few months ago, in May 2010, a plate which had been left shut in the microwave was found in pieces on the floor. Also very recently, a sales assistant was having her lunch when the tap suddenly came on by itself. When she went to turn it off, she could see the handle moving and the water stopped. In the same room, the kettle has been known to come on by itself. The tap, kettle and socket were checked but no fault was found.

Until fairly recently Lulu's activities were confined to the basement area and the staff were able to cope with this, but the intruder alarm on the shop floor has gone off several times over the last few months. There is never any sign of a break in and nothing has been stolen, but jewellery displays have been knocked over. Perhaps most frightening was the day when a pen box was seen to rise from a table in the shop and fly rapidly past a sales assistant's head as if someone had thrown it. Perhaps 'Lulu' is more unfriendly than previously thought!

Guildhall

Exeter Guildhall dates back to 1200 and is the oldest municipal building still in use in Britain. Trials were once held in the Guildhall and prisoners, including children, awaiting trial were chained in the basement in foul, cold conditions. Water leaked in from a nearby damaged water cistern and

Exeter Guildhall and Ernest Jones Jeweller's.

many prisoners became seriously ill with pneumonia before their trials could take place. Stale bread and water were provided only three times a week. In 1829, a clergyman complained about the conditions, but Mayor Robert Rigers Sanders' only comment was that a place of punishment was not supposed to be comfortable.

In 1920, the ghost of a girl in a dirty long dress was seen walking across the floor. She seemed to have no feet. This was explained by the fact that the floor used to be lower, but had been raised during some maintenance work in the early 1900s.

Although staff at the Guildhall today report few spooky experiences, the ghost of a large black dog has been seen. It sits in the corner of the Main Hall carefully watching everyone. It is possible that the animal was once used as a Guildhall guard dog.

Guildhall Shopping Centre

A strange smell of roses has been noticed in the basement of the shopping centre. The aroma is nauseating and so strong that it makes people feel ill. The smell heralds the appearance of a ghost. She is dressed in 1940s style clothing. The woman wanders around the basement as if looking for something before shaking her head sadly and promptly disappearing. The sickly smell disappears as quickly as she does.

Thinking that the date of the woman's clothing might be a clue I did more research and found that the area had never been bombed. Nor was there a building there in the 1940s. Before the shopping centre was built, the land was a car park for many years.

JJB Sports

This building was once a store called Webbers but in 1919 there was a terrible fire which destroyed the interior.

Fortunately no one was inside at the time, but falling debris killed a man and his dog who were walking nearby. None of the staff at JJB Sports have experienced any ghostly events, but the *Exeter Herald* of 24 August 1986 reported that the hazy image of a man and a dog have been seen several times outside the building.

Lakeland Homeware

Lakeland Homeware is located in a building which dates from around 1650 and was once a merchant's house. Now a department store, staff in the shop report that there is a strangely uneasy feel to the cellar. On a number of occasions they have found their carefully arranged stock in disarray. At first this was put down to delivery men being clumsy or not knowing where items are usually stored. Then it was realised that the basement was often disrupted on days when delivery the men had not been in the shop. The ladies in Lakeland believe that there is a poltergeist in the cellar. The spook seems to particularly dislike anything to do with microwaves and freezers as dishes, containers and utensils associated with these seem to be targeted most often.

Laura Ashley

Caroline has worked at the store for years. She says she is quite sceptical about ghosts, but finds the place, 'A bit creepy, especially if I hear whispering and no one else seems to be near.'

Though nothing strange happens on the ground floor, staff have reported being inexplicably overcome by feelings of terror while on the first floor. This is followed by doors and drawers opening and closing on their own. Occasionally there are loud noises as if someone is moving furniture. This usually happens early in the morning when the shop is first unlocked and it is

The upper floor of Laura Ashley.

not possible for anyone to be there. Several times, staff members have been into the shops on either side to find out if anyone has been moving large objects and have been told that no one has.

Perhaps even more strange was the wallpaper rack. Several staff on the floor have observed rolls of wallpaper gradually poke out of the rack as if someone was pulling them. This was initially put down to the effects of a loose floorboard. However, when the rack was replaced, the floorboard was fixed. Today, the new shelving holds a display or ornamental candles which fall to the floor for no apparent reason.

While doing a stock audit alone one night on the ground floor in the 1990s, the manageress, Jackie, was scared to hear footsteps, laughing and banging from the first floor. In a panic she called the police, who could find nothing wrong. Their dog however, usually an obedient well-trained animal, refused to go into the upstairs front of the building.

Lush

None of the staff at Lush are happy to go into the basement alone. One of the ladies, Kerri, took me to have a look. The stairs leading down to the basement are painted in pale green and yellow, the colours of the company's logo. Normally this would be quite cheery, but the atmosphere on the stairs was surprisingly gloomy and oppressive. At the basement door Kerri stopped, saying, 'I only ever go in there if I absolutely have to.'

The temperature dropped as I stepped through the door. Although I had been warned about this I was still surprised at how much colder it had suddenly become. A sense of dread inexplicably overtook me, but I made myself walk round the room taking photographs. Back upstairs other staff members told me that no matter how carefully stock is stacked in the basement, things constantly go missing – only to be found in odd places.

Marks & Spencer

The shop, which is a modern building, is said to be built on an old Roman burial ground. This may explain some of the ghostly happenings in the store.

The foreboding basement storeroom at Lush Soaps.

There is some poltergeist activity, particularly in the storage area where tools often disappear; this is very annoying for the staff who have work to do. More alarming are the rustling and scraping sounds which have been heard by staff when they are alone.

Annoying poltergeist activity is not confined to the storeroom. Staff in the Food Hall report that sometimes when they arrive in the morning they find packets and boxes strewn around the floor. Food displays are constructed so that they won't fall over on their own and careful shop security means that no one could possibly be in the Food Hall overnight.

A member of the administration team refused to stay in the offices if no one else was with her. She had heard strange scraping noises accompanied by the sound of whispering one night while working late. Believing that she was imagining things, the lady wasn't worried at first. Then on another evening an unseen entity pushed her violently, grabbed her pencil and notebook and hurled them across the room. While this was happening the air suddenly went very cold with a breeze seeming to come from nowhere.

The Roman Soldier, High Street
I became interested in the supernatural after reading the works of a local writer, the late Theo Brown. This story from her appeared in the 'Report and Transactions' of the Devonshire Association for the Advancement of Science, Literature and the Arts' in 1983:

> In 1981 Theo was having her hair cut in a High Street salon when one of the hairdressers told her that the premises were haunted. Theo was immediately intrigued and asked for more details. She was told that ghosts in Roman soldier's uniforms

had been seen by several of the salon workers and that there were often footsteps and strange creaking sounds from the empty cellar. Theo took the claims seriously as the manageress complained that in spite of high unemployment levels it was becoming difficult to keep staff.

Thornton's
A poltergeist has been known to tip chocolates out of their boxes and bang on the shop walls. Footsteps can often be heard overhead when no one is upstairs and the toilet door opens and closes by itself, even while a staff member is in it. The ladies who work at Thornton's seem unconcerned by their otherworldly visitor as there is a pleasant atmosphere in the shop. The only problem they have is that chocolate which the spook has tipped onto the floor cannot be sold!

The Turks Head
There has been a pub on this sight for over 500 years. Its name is said to have originated from Turkish prisoners who were housed there before execution. Charles Dickens was a frequent customer at the Turks Head in the 1840s when visiting his parents who lived near Exeter. It is said that he gained inspiration for some of his famous characters by watching the antics of the pub regulars.

A thin, bearded man in Victorian dress has been seen outside the Turks head. Could this be the ghost of the famous writer?

A red-haired woman haunts the Turks head. She has been seen wandering around the bar as if looking for something that is no longer there. Mrs Peterson, a former barmaid, has seen her several times and believes that she was the mistreated wife of a former landlord who was a violent drunk. The unfortunate woman committed

The Turks Head.

and the upper floors were a bar and club used by navy personnel. This was supposed to shut at midnight, but sailors being sailors, it often stayed open much later.

On a number of occasions club members, who were locking up downstairs, reported hearing banging and shouting coming from inside the building. At first it was assumed that someone had been left inside and the doors were reopened to investigate. No one was ever found. The noises always occurred at 2 a.m.

Responsibility for locking up fell to different people each night. Even so, the story of the strange noises spread. Eventually someone decided to look into the history of the building. It was discovered that the recruitment centre was on the site of a building which had been completely demolished during the bombing of May 1942. The occupants of the building had tragically all been found dead at 2 a.m.

Celly's Hair Salon has only been open for about a year. The previous owner ran a lighting shop from the premises and told me that he had never had any strange experiences in the shop. I approached the ladies working in Celly's without much hope of being able to add to the story. Not only had the spooky happenings seemed to have stopped, but the salon is light and modern. I had to remind myself that ghosts don't always live in ancient buildings!

It turned out to be worth my visit. When I relayed the building's ghost story to them they told me that they hadn't heard it before. Then one of them said, 'Mind you, I wouldn't be surprised if it is haunted. There are always strange scraping noises in here that we can't explain – like heavy old furniture being moved and we haven't even got any!'

Her colleague added, 'Then there are the running footsteps when no one is there and

suicide, but likes to return to the pub for a drink! The optics have been seen to operate by themselves on a number of occasions.

'She used to really startle me,' Mrs Peterson said. 'But in spite of that I felt sorry for her.'

Today the building is still called Turks Head, but now houses Prezzo's Italian restaurant. A waiter told me that in rooms on an upper floor there is a terrible atmosphere. A vivid light which looks like a pair of eyes has been seen to flash on the wall. Sometimes an unpleasant smell accompanies the light. After only a few seconds the light and smell fade.

Celly's Hair Salon, Sidwell Street

In 1974, my friend Colin was in the Royal Navy Auxiliary Service. Back then the building, which now houses Celly's Hair Salon, was the Royal Navy Recruitment Centre. The ground floor was used for interviews and naval careers information the horrible feeling in the storeroom. Do you think they're ghosts from the Second World War?'

Stephens' Café, Sidwell Street

Michael Evans is a former General Secretary of Exeter's Spiritualist Church. Several years ago Michael and his colleague John, a very experienced trance-medium ,conducted an investigation at Stephens' Café which had been built over a bombed site from the Second World War. Several female staff members were refusing to use the staffroom complaining that they had seen a strange ghostly shape hovering about and that there was an uncomfortable atmosphere. John made an initial visit and confirmed that there was definitely something there; so a full investigation was arranged. John, seated in the staffroom, went into a trance and the voice of a young boy came through. He explained that he had been killed during the bombing of 1942 and was looking for his parents.

John asked, 'Would you like to join your Mum and Dad? They'd love to see you.'

The boy replied, 'That's why I keep coming back here'.

Michael then said, 'We will ask if your mum can come. She can explain things, and help you on to a lovely place where you will be happy.'

The boy said, 'Yes, I see her. It is my mother! She has been looking for me as I have been looking for her.'

Michael asked, 'Will you go with her now?'

The boy emphatically answered, 'I will go with her. Yes!'

When John explained that his appearance was frightening the people who now worked in the building, the boy said, 'You can tell your ladies that there will be no more shadows in the night. Goodbye!'

Michael explained to me that the boy and his parents had been on two different levels and John had provided the link to enable them to reunite. Michael asked the manageress to let him know what happened and after a few weeks she told him that the ghostly shape had not returned and her workers were happily enjoying the 'normal' atmosphere of their staffroom again.

Today Stoke's Greengrocers occupies the approximate site of Stephens' Café. No one has seen anything unusual inside the shop, but there have been reports of a strange flickering shadow moving up and down the street outside.

3

Castle Quarter

EXETER'S Castle Quarter has been witness to a fair amount of grisly history. For many years in the Old Courts at Exeter castle judges handed down dreadful punishments before unfortunate prisoners were dragged off to nearby cells to await their fate. Most tourists visiting the Castle Quarter make their way to Southernhay Gardens, a very pleasant area of parkland. Here they enjoy the open space and admire the beautiful plants. Few know of the ghostly activities that take place in the area.

The Hole in the Wall Pub, Little Castle Street

The Hole in the Wall was built as the old County Prison in the sixteenth century. The famous Bideford witches, Temperance Lloyd, Susannah Edwards and Mary Trembles were held here after being sentenced to death for witchcraft in August 1682. They were among the last people to be executed for this 'crime' in England. Today a plaque to their memory can be seen on the wall of nearby Rougemont Castle.

The prison was described as 'a living tomb, a sink of filth' by the Revd Miles, a local vicar who was horrified to hear that many of its prisoners died of disease or starvation. The doctor in charge of prisons refused to visit in case he too became ill. After public protest the prison was demolished in 1785. When the dungeon ceiling was broken up local residents reported hearing three ghostly female voices and screams echoing out of the underground cells. A clergyman hurriedly organised prayer meetings at the site, set to last for twelve days. The unearthly shrieking continued until the evening of the last day when everything suddenly became quiet and it was declared that the tormented souls, believed to be those of the Bideford Witches, had at last entered heaven.

When I visited one of the barmaids told me that strange noises are often heard on the lower floors where the cells used to be, though as far as she knows, no one has seen anything spooky recently.

Northernhay Gardens

These L-shaped gardens sit around the outside of a corner of Exeter's Roman city wall. Although much of the wall has been altered and rebuilt over the centuries, it is possible to see the finest remaining Roman section here. Unsurprisingly the gardens are said to be haunted by various spooks. Dubious stories of ghostly apparitions in 'Roman' uniforms go back many years. However, I became less sceptical about the haunted status of Rougemont Gardens when I heard the following story.

In 2003, a young man called James climbed over the locked park gate one night to steal some plants which he hoped to sell.

'I was only sixteen,' he told me, 'and it was a bit scary, but my mates egged me on.'

As James dug he heard his friends shout and saw them running away. Suddenly something hit James on the back of the head and he fell forwards. He then felt something pulling his feet. Twisting round he saw the figure of a man.

'He was wearing sort of vicar's robes and I could see a cross. My first thought was that I was going to be in a lot of trouble from my Dad, as I'd being caught stealing before, so I wriggled round and managed to escape.'

James ran to the gate and climbed over before looking back.

'The 'vicar' was still there. I heard him shout. "Repent and you will be forgiven!"'

'I'm not religious.' James said. 'And normally I would have had a real laugh about it later, but the vicar suddenly just disappeared!'

I asked James what he made of the experience.

'Well, I definitely saw it, but my mates didn't and really took the mickey,' he said. 'We were a bit of a rough lot, but I've never stolen anything since.'

The Old Courts, Exeter Castle
After the Monmouth Rebellion of 1685 the infamous 'Hanging Judge' Jeffries passed judgement on twelve of the rebels at Exeter Castle. They were sentenced to be hanged, drawn and quartered.

Jeffries is said to haunt the castle in the form of a black pig. Though no one would have been brave enough to say it to his face, 'The Black Pig' was Jefferies' nickname! Over the years there have been a number of stories about people seeing a large black animal in the castle grounds late at night. It could perhaps be dismissed as a stray dog, but on being approached the creature is seen to have a strange hairless face and will suddenly disappear into thin air.

In the eighteenth and nineteenth centuries the castle employed gatekeepers. Although it was an easy way to make a living and regular work was hard to find, they never seemed to stay in their jobs for long. In 1792 an old chapel in the castle grounds was removed to make way for a new gatekeeper's lodge. This had very comfortable accommodation, but still employees left soon after starting their jobs. One complained that there were ghostly men on the stairs, with terrible injuries. Another departed hurriedly with his family in the middle of the night after hearing ghostly moaning, wailing and tapping accompanied by a horrible smell.

In 1891, during renovations, the floor of the lodge was dug out down to the level of the old chapel. Here eleven skeletons were found. One was that of a large man who had died from a blow which had shattered his skull. It is thought that the hidden skeletons were prisoners from the nearby jail who had died at the hands of the prison guards.

Old Telephone Exchange, Castle Street
The old telephone exchange is located between Musgrave Road and the Central Library. One evening in 1949 the night-watchman was meticulously checking the building over in anticipation of the

Old Courts, Exeter Castle.

The old telephone exchange.

43

Courtyard at Timepiece Club.

arrival of Princess Elizabeth (now Queen Elizabeth II). She was expected at the Telephone Exchange the next day as part of her visit to the city.

During his rounds a series of heavy doors along a corridor suddenly banged shut then opened again for no apparent reason. Footsteps could be heard running along the corridor, but no one was there. The night-watchman was not given to nervous fancies. He called the police, suspecting that an intruder had entered the building (which could be a serious security breech due to the royal visit). The police made a thorough search of the building, but no intruder was found. After the police left, the watchman went back to his room and settled down with a cup of tea to while away his shift. Suddenly, the door behind him suddenly banged open again and he felt something grab his arm, though no one was there. After this the watchman made a hasty retreat!

There are, of course, records of Princess Elizabeth's visit, though no mention is made of the Telephone Exchange. Perhaps it was hastily removed from her itinerary after the frightening events of the night before.

Timepiece Club, Little Castle Street

The courtyard of this old pub is built on the site of an ancient burial ground. Gravestones, removed when the building was constructed, decorate the walls of the courtyard giving it a very eerie atmosphere.

In the 1980s more old graves were discovered under the flagstones when renovations were carried out. Strange and very strong floral smells lasting for just a few seconds accompanied the removal of each gravestone. Workmen complained that their tools, carefully locked away at the end of the day, were found next morning scattered around the building site even though the foreman had the only key.

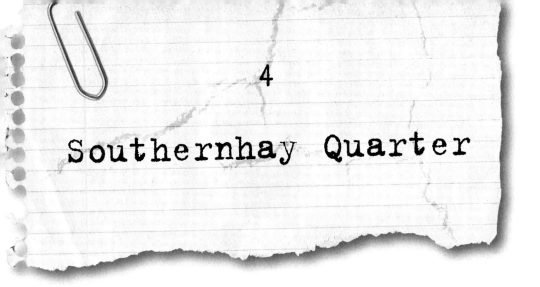

4

Southernhay Quarter

SOUTHERNHAY is an area of very fine four-storey Georgian buildings. They once housed the wealthiest residents of Exeter who moved from their once fashionable houses in the city centre to escape the dirt, smells and noise. The beautiful gardens which run along the centre of Southernhay belie the terrible activities which once took place and the ghostly experiences many people have had in the area.

The Barnfield Theatre, Barnfield Road

The Barnfield Theatre was built in 1891 and was among the earliest to present film shows from 1906. Today the Barnfield presents a very varied programme of drama, comedy and music.

I met theatre manager, Julie, who showed me around backstage and told me about the Barnfield's ghosts. The building is so haunted that there have been several investigations by paranormal groups and clairvoyants who have presented shows; these have uncovered three ghosts resident in the building.

Julie has appeared on the Barnfield stage several times. During a production of *Far From the Maddening Crowd* she noticed a very nasty smell coming from the left wing. When another cast member went to investigate he found the area unusually cold. The smell suddenly disappeared and very quickly the temperature rose.

In another play a chess set was used as a prop. At the end of each performance it was stored in a large Chinese takeaway box. One day the box disappeared just before the play began. Another chess set was hastily found. During the last performance, when fake snow was thrown from the 'fly' floor above the stage, the box containing the chess set fell out of the snow box and hit Julie on the head. Thankfully she was not seriously hurt. No one could explain how the box came to be hidden in the fake snow.

The fly floor is used by stage hands when raising or lowering scenery. Julie refused to accompany me there. She said, 'It's really creepy. No one likes it up there. Let me know how it makes you feel.'

I was later able to tell her that I thought there was a strange and threatening atmosphere. In fact, it was the scariest place I visited during my research! Julie then told me that while doing a show a visiting clairvoyant has contacted a ghost named

'Murphy' on the fly floor. It is thought that he was once a theatre volunteer. On one occasion the rope used for lowering scenery stuck and though the stagehand pulled as hard as possible it would not move. Suddenly he felt someone behind him tugging on the rope, which freed it. He turned round to thank the helper but no one was there. Was this 'Murphy' lending a hand?

In November 2009 *Oh! What a Lovely War* was staged. In this play poppies were thrown from the fly floor to land on stage. After the production all the poppies were cleared away. During rehearsals for the next play, some weeks later, two of the cast had a serious row on stage. The director made them apologise to each other; as they did a single poppy fluttered down. No one was on the fly floor at the time.

'Mary Jane' is a ghost who sits in the stalls and watches rehearsals. Regular performers are unfazed by her, but she has caused quite a stir among new people. I took some photographs of the stalls from the stage. Though quite dark, the air was clear and I had an uninterrupted view. The photographs reveal a number of strange spots and shapes. As my camera is digital, this can't be blamed on bad film and several photographs from different angles revealed the same results.

A strange pink light has been seen on stage during rehearsals. A clairvoyant established that this is the ghost of 'Denton', a one-time actor at the Barnfield. He is very effeminate and his behaviour is naughty – he likes to mess about with the props, hiding them or leaving them in the wrong place.

Several years ago council workers were employed to fix the boiler. One put a ladder against the wall to reach some high pipes. The ladder suddenly flew across the room and the terrified men fled. Some time later the theatre employed carpenters to rebuild the stage. As they worked they kept hearing footsteps but no one was there. It seems that one of the resident ghosts objects to changes to the building!

As with any organisation people at the Barnfield have the occasional moan or disagreement. One of the office staff told me that whenever this happens the bell on the reception desk changes tone without anyone altering it. Sometimes shows have a religious content and the reception desk bell goes off by itself again.

Holloway Street

There is archaeological evidence of buildings and a graveyard from the Roman period in the vicinity of Holloway Street, though today it is an area of large Victorian Houses, many of which have now been converted into flats. Jack has lived in one of these for thirty years. During this time he has experienced a number of strange happenings.

Though no one else lives there, Jack has often smelled Wintergreen, commonly dispensed in the Victorian period as a pain killer. The smell will suddenly occur, grow stronger then fade away down the hall as if an unseen person has walked past. A visiting cousin was repeatedly nudged as if someone was clapping her on the shoulder when she walked along the hall. Then, in 2004, a friend was tidying her hair in the hall mirror when she saw the reflection of a man behind her. She was very shocked but remembered that his clothes were old-fashioned like those worn by people before the First World War. The lady has flatly refused to visit since this happened.

Jack has no plans to move. He says it is possible that his ghostly lodger actually saved his life. Jack had always been very fit and enjoyed sport, so one day, feeling a little

The stalls at the Barnfield Theatre.

Fly floor at the Barnfield Theatre.

47

unwell, he wasn't worried, but decided to have a lie down. He had begun to feel better when he heard the words 'hospital' and 'urgently' whispered several times.

'I began to feel dizzy and sick so I phoned for an ambulance,' Jack told me. 'The next thing I knew, I was in a hospital and had survived a massive heart attack.' The paramedics had reached him just in time. Since then, Jack, has researched the history of the house and discovered that during the Victorian period it belonged to a doctor who had a surgery and small dispensary on the ground floor, reached by the hall.

Hotel Barcelona, Magdalen Street

The Hotel Barcelona, opened in 2001, was originally built as an eye hospital. It opened a century before, in 1901.

Hotel Barcelona.

Miss Kinninmont was the first matron of the hospital. She was very dedicated to her work and was a keen fundraiser for the infirmary. Influential visitors, who might be a source of funds often asked to see the wards. Matron Kinninmont was always the person to show them around. When not acting as tour-guide her working day was spent on the third floor – the ward for the most serious cases.

Since opening as Hotel Barcelona many of the hotel maids refuse to go into the rooms on the upper floors alone and one claimed to have seen 'Matron Kinnimont' – a woman in a long dress and nurse's hat on the landing.

I visited the hotel in 2007 and went to the Kino Bar for a meal. Despite the modern, bustling surroundings, I found the place to be really creepy. Although I hadn't started research for this book, I asked one of barmaids if she'd ever seen anything spooky. She told me that no one would work in the Kino Bar alone on quiet nights after a barmaid had twice seen a woman in a nurse's

uniform in the mirror. The barmaid turned quickly, but the figure had gone. Other staff members reported suddenly smelling strong antiseptic on several occasions.

The hotel has been closed for refurbishment since 2008, but a shadowy figure has been reported in a third-floor bedroom window late at night. Security guards have investigated, but found no one.

The Old Royal Devon and Exeter Hospital, Southernhay

Unlike the other fine buildings on Southernhay, the hospital is forbidding and dismal. Though tourists in their hundreds take photographs of the area every year, few pause for long outside this ugly structure.

The Devon and Exeter Hospital was founded by Cathedral Dean Alured Clarke in 1743. The Dean was very frail and died aged forty-six a year before the hospital opened. A sickly-looking man in eighteenth-century costume was often seen walking in and out of hospital rooms gazing around. It has been claimed that this was the ghost of Alured Clarke admiring the hospital he did not get chance to see in his lifetime.

Beer was brewed in the basement of the hospital; each patient being allowed three pints a day, which would have been a useful addition to their diet and was safer to drink than the polluted local water. Several of the ladies who were patrons of the hospital were known to disapprove of alcohol. The brewery was eventually closed down and turned into a storage area.

Few of the young nurses would venture down there alone because a lady in an elaborate long dress was seen on several occasions. At first it was thought that she was a visitor who had lost her way. On being addressed, however, she would shake her head angrily before seeming to disappear – leaving a distinct chill in the air. Many hospital staff were convinced that she was the ghost of one of the disapproving patrons.

In the 1970s the shadowy figure of a nurse in Victorian uniform was often seen entering the intensive care department and pausing by the patient's beds. On being asked by a staff member what she wanted, the figure would suddenly disappear. She was also seen pacing the hospital corridors. When members of staff tried to speak to her she would ignore them. Another nurse once tried to touch the ghost, but her hand went right through her arm.

On many occasions the 'Grey Nurse' was seen rearranging the flowers of sleeping patients into the shape of a cross. This was bad news as the patient always died soon

The old Royal Devon and Exeter Hospital.

after – even those who had recovered from their illness and were awaiting discharge!

Less ominous was the little girl in Edwardian dress who would often sit on the beds of elderly patients cheerfully chatting to them. At first it was thought that she must be the child of another visitor. However, she began to appear at all times of the day and it was realised that she was, in fact, a ghost. The same child was sometimes seen in one of the corridors playing with a bat and ball.

In the 1970s, just before the hospital moved to a new site, a young theatre technician felt that someone was standing behind him as he prepared equipment. Turning, he saw a naked body bearing the marks of a crude operation. Very shaken, the technician told his colleagues. Instead of the expected teasing, he was told that the horrible apparition had been seen several times before and was thought to be the ghost of an unfortunate patient from a time when surgical practices were very crude.

The old hospital is disused at present and unfortunately I was unable to gain entry for health and safety reasons. The building is going to be converted into flats and I am awaiting the arrival of the first new tenants with interest. Will they also see the strange and frightening apparitions?

Southernhay Gardens

For centuries executions took place on what is now Southernhay Gardens. My friend Colin, a city Redcoat guide, told me that the gallows were near the giant Luscombe Oak which can still be seen today.

In 1998 on a sunlit afternoon a man was crossing Southernhay when he saw three young men in very old style clothing. He noticed them because one was being dragged by the other two. As the man watched, the struggling victim screamed. The man was about to intervene when he realised that the three youths cast only two shadows and that they had a strangely transparent appearance. The man hurried away. As he looked back the boys suddenly disappeared into thin air.

Very early one morning following a snowfall in the winter of 2003, two men walking across Southernhay heard screaming close behind them, though no one else was about. They looked round and saw three sets of footprints in the snow. When they looked at the same place again, there were only two sets of prints and marks suggesting that something had been pulled along the ground. The men hurried on and the screaming stopped.

In the days when executions were carried out at Southernhay, victims were driven in carts along the nearby road before being dragged to the gallows.

Southgate Hotel, Southernhay

Interestingly, the haunted activity at the Southgate Hotel takes place in the modern extension which was built in 1989. Perhaps this can be explained by the fact that the new foundations disturbed a long-forgotten graveyard which may well have been there when the original hotel was built in the 1800s. Research has shown that the burial site belonged to the nearby Holy Trinity Church and many victims of the cholera outbreak of 1832 were buried there.

A strange old cart has been seen in the hotel car park on a number of occasions by people walking on the public footpath behind the hotel. People in the car park who are alerted to the cart's presence can't see it.

Inside the new part of the hotel, staff working alone regularly hear strange shuffling noises as if something is being dragged along the floor behind them. One night a porter, who has since changed jobs, heard sobbing and cries of 'No, no!' coming from a storeroom. When he checked no one was there, but the sobbing noise continued, before gradually fading.

Southgate Prison, South Street

Strange howling noises have been heard in the early hours near the site where the city's Southgate once stood. However, there are no buildings nearby which are occupied at night and so nothing to explain these haunting screams.

The towers of Exeter's Southgate were a prison for many years. During the 1770s John Barnes was the landlord of the Black Horse, which was located near Southgate. In his youth Barnes had been a rogue, but he changed when he married his religious wife and had a large family. Unfortunately, money worries caused him to fall back into his old ways.

In 1777, Barnes and two accomplices robbed a coach on its way from Exeter to London. Barnes only agreed to take part on condition that no one was hurt, but to his horror a child was killed during the raid. All three robbers were incarcerated in Southgate Prison to await execution. A number of Exeter residents pleaded for leniency for Barnes because of his good character, but this was refused. During an escape attempt his two accomplices killed the young son of the jailer. They got away but Barnes, who had stopped to try to save the boy, was caught. Loud weeping and praying was heard coming from Southgate Prison night and day as Barnes awaited his execution, which took place in 1778.

The Southgate and its prison were demolished in 1819, but its location is marked by yellow bricks in the pavement.

Wynyard's Hospital, Magdalen Street

The hospital, opposite the Hotel Barcelona, was founded in 1435 by William Wynard to care for the poor of the area. Unfortunately, many were so ill and malnourished by the time they were admitted that they didn't survive. A pale old man dressed in a ragged coat is said to wander nearby late at night. Passers-by have been alarmed to see him fall down, but when they run to offer assistance there is nothing there but the strong smell of rotting flesh.

5

West Quarter

TODAY Exeter's West Quarter is a lively cosmopolitan area of the city with many bars and restaurants. Until the late eighteenth century, the West Quarter was part of the city's manufacturing area and the workers were crammed into unhealthy slums where disease was rife. In the early part of the twentieth century there was a large scale slum clearance in the West Quarter, though many old buildings remain to give the area its character – its ghost stories!

St Bartholomew's Cemetery

The cemetery was opened in 1835 as other burial sites in the area had become full following the cholera outbreak of 1832.

A ghostly black dog has been seen walking alone past the cemetery in Exe Street on many occasions. The dog stops suddenly, throws back its head and howls, but no sound is heard. Legend has it that the day after each sighting someone in the Exe Street area dies.

There are other variations on this story. In the 1880s a strange blue light, like a flickering flame, was seen in the cemetery several times late at night hovering over the gravestones. The light then floated over the roofs of houses in the locality; whenever this happened one the inhabitants died shortly afterwards. Usually the victim had exhibited no signs of ill health and one wonders whether hearing the legend actually scared the poor victims to death!

A strange apparition in the cemetery frightens courting couples at dusk. The figure is a man in old-fashioned clothes with hideous injuries to his face. He staggers about screaming loudly before falling down and promptly disappearing.

Bartholomew's Cemetery has not been used for many years now. Fortunately, no one seems to succumb to the threat of the blue flame these days, but the disfigured man was last seen in as late as the 1990s.

I visited the cemetery to take photographs. As you'd expect it is an unsettling place, but I busied myself with my digital camera equipment trying to get a good shot of the gravestones. Many have fallen and it was quite hard to get an angle showing stones standing up. Eventually I managed to get a frame showing about seven gravestones, one of which had a very large cross. I spotted a squirrel in a tree and took a picture of that too.

When I looked for the saved photographs a few minutes later the shot of the graves was missing, but the squirrel picture was there. Thinking I'd accidentally pressed delete somehow, I retook the grave picture. Again it didn't save. While standing on the same spot I took a picture of other graves in the opposite direction which saved without any problem. When I turned round to take the first shot again I couldn't get more than two graves in the frame and the stone with the cross wasn't there. At this point I decided to leave!

Later I returned with a friend and we both scoured the entire cemetery but could see no stone cross anywhere.

Bartholomew Street

In the summer of 1960, George was an Exeter schoolboy. His friend's family had moved into a house in the West Quarter. It had been empty for some years and needed a lot of work so the two boys had volunteered to tidy the front garden. While they were moving rubbish, George's friend happened to glance through front door (which was open due to the hot weather). A dim figure was climbing the stairs with one arm on the banister. Seeing his friend point, George looked in the same direction just as the figure paused and turned round.

I asked George to describe the figure and he said, 'It was blurry. You could dimly see through it to the stairs behind. Even though the ghost seemed to be waving in a friendly way we were shocked at first.'

His friend's family lived in the house for several years and got used to the strange apparition which, they decided, meant them no harm.

'The stairs were always cold, though,' George told me. 'Even when my friend's Dad had radiators installed and going full blast, the stairs were always freezing cold though there were no draughts.'

Chevalier Inn, 79 Fore Street

During the Civil War, the inn got its name because it was the drinking den of the Cavaliers. It is said that King Charles I himself was once hidden from his Roundhead enemies at the Chevalier. The inn was the location of numerous duels. Often these skirmishes were friendly rough-housing which got out of hand! Sadly, the original inn was one of the wonderful buildings destroyed during the Blitz. Only a section of its wall remained and this was incorporated into the replacement building which was constructed in the 1950s.

On dark nights, a figure in Cavalier costume with a stomach wound pouring blood has been seen by the old wall. Staff at the Chevalier hate the attic storeroom as a seriously injured ghostly man has been seen up there. Usually staff members make a swift exit from the room! It is plausible that the original building's attic was used in secret to treat soldiers after duelling bouts which were against army rules.

City Gate Hotel, North Street

A previous landlord hanged himself in the pub's kitchen and cats belonging to subsequent tenants have been seen to spit and shake upon approaching the spot.

Built in the early nineteenth century, the pub has a cellar dating from the medieval period. Over the years many people have reported feeling that they were being watched while in the cellar. Though the skylight is firmly closed a cold wind sometimes blows through even if it is warm and windless outside. In 1991 a séance was organised by a group of students. They left pretty quickly at three am after their Ouija board unaccountably flew through the air when no one was touching it. As they ran for the stairs they heard ghostly screaming coming from the cellar accompanied by the howling of a dog.

Three o'clock in the morning seems to be the 'witching hour' for this establishment! This is when strange unearthly music has been heard accompanied by the lights flicking on and off by themselves.

Conservatory Restaurant, North Street

This timber-framed building on North Street dates from the Tudor Period. During the early 1900s, the front of the building was completely changed. This involved the removal of some of the Tudor framework and its replacement with brick. On a number of occasions the shadowy figure of a strangely dressed man has been seen staring at the restaurant late at night and shaking his head. Locals believe that he was a proud former owner of the building when it was still a very smart private townhouse 500 years ago.

Lee Terrace

On Lee Terrace is a house haunted by a very angry ghost. Since before the First World War, residents of the house have been frightened by the spirit who has pushed people and upset pets. Alarmingly, in one of the bedrooms the ghost causes the doors of a built-in cupboard to open and shut violently. Few tenants have stayed in the house long.

In 1895 a murder was committed at Lee Terrace and details appeared in the *Exeter Evening Post* of 29 August under the headline, 'Wife Murdered in Chilling Attack'. Details in the article are sketchy and the woman is not named, but readers were informed that she was killed by her jealous husband who slit her throat because he suspected her of being unfaithful. After the murder her husband began to panic and hid his wife's body in a bedroom cupboard, where it was later discovered by police.

Rack Street

In the 1950s, the ghost of a weaver singing as he operated his loom, at all hours of the night, could be heard in the West Quarter. This was long after the weaving of cloth in the city had stopped as a commercial concern. Eventually the noise was traced to a derelict building which was empty and had been firmly locked up for a number of years. People in nearby houses were alarmed at the ghostly sound and annoyed at being kept awake at night when they themselves had to be up early for work and so a priest was called in.

At first he was very sceptical about the resident's claims, but he soon changed his mind after searching the building himself and spending a night in one of the local's houses where he too heard the unearthly noise. It was decided that the priest should conduct a service in the derelict building. As he began to pray there was a loud banging and scraping. The prayer was finished by the priest sprinkling consecrated soil from Cathedral Green all over the floor. Then he went outside and continued spreading it around the house walls. This did the trick and the ghostly neighbour was silenced.

Smythen Street

Evan & Gadd Chemists was once a well-known Smythen Street shop. The following story was covered in the *Exeter Weekly News* on 7 September 1980.

Miss Joyce Maunder (who was a well respected assistant at the chemist's) frequently saw the ghost of a delivery man who had sadly collapsed and died while he was lifting a box of heavy bottles in the shop. Miss Maunder was known to be very religious and colleagues didn't pay much attention to her claims at first. Then they too began to see him. After a while the shop ladies got used to his appearances. Unfortunately he had been very conscientious about his work and his ghost continued the annoying habit of constantly tidying things away while they were still being used.

St Nicholas Priory, Off Fore Street

Like many other religious establishments the Priory was partly destroyed by Henry VIII during the Dissolution of the

St Nicholas Priory.

Monasteries in 1530s. The building was then given to a wealthy Tudor family who were supporters of Henry. They turned it into a beautiful townhouse which was one of the most elegant in Exeter. Today St Nicholas' is a museum of Tudor Life.

According to a former attendant, the Great Hall of the building on the first floor was haunted by a monk until the ghost was banished during a secret exorcism in the early 1980s. Spectral monks are still said to haunt the exterior of the building and locals claim to have seen them disappearing through walls.

St Olaves Hotel, Mary Arches Street

Over the years the St Olaves building was used for a variety of purposes and the ghostly activity here reflects this. It was built as a townhouse for a wealthy business family in 1827. Recently one of the receptionists told me that later in the century the building became a home for unmarried mothers. Interestingly this fact may explain the ghostly apparition of a woman in a long dress. She walks backwards and forwards in front of the hotel in a distressed state carrying a small baby.

The building was altered extensively when it was converted into a hotel. After taking down an upper floor, a builder was alarmed to see an aged man standing high up with nothing supporting his feet. The builder quickly fetched a ladder, but when he returned the old man had vanished, though there was no way down.

Poltergeist activity has occurred in part of the hotel which used to be the stables. Items have been broken inexplicably and furniture has been moved.

St Olave's Hotel.

In the building which was once a stable block a friendly waving ghost has been seen. Guests in room No. 16 of the hotel have, on several occasions, reported that they were gently hugged by unseen arms.

Starz Bar, Lower North Street

This bar has a very hazardous and unwelcoming poltergeist in the basement! Whenever alterations have been carried out strange moaning sounds have been heard accompanied by tools suddenly flying through the air as if thrown by unseen hands. In the early 1900s, a tragedy occurred when a fire in the basement killed the owner's two children. Starz Bar staff, who have noticed that one corner of the basement gets inexplicably hot, are convinced that the tool-throwing ghost is the children's distraught father.

Today the basement is a smart lounge bar. Few customers would imagine that it was the site of such tragedy, though many have been puzzled to hear the sound of children laughing. There is definitely a strange atmosphere, particularly at one end of the bar where customers have often complained that they have felt someone punching their shoulder when no one else is near.

Occasionally, the shadowy figure of an old man has been seen outside the building pacing up and down as if in a panic. Is he is the ghost of the dead children's father waiting in the vain hope that his children might be rescued?

The White Hart Hotel, South Street

The charming White Hart dates from the fourteenth century and is one of the most haunted buildings in the city. The White Hart is my favourite Exeter pub, though my claim to fame as a visitor is not as spectacular as those of snooker player Steve Davis and the Monty Python team, who have all stayed at the hotel!

In the 1640s, a workman went down the well at the White Hart to investigate a foul smell. He did not return, so another man went down to look for him. Neither were ever seen again. Investigations proved that there were no bodies in the well. The terrible smell was said to emanate from a cockatrice, a ghostly cross between a cockerel and a serpent. So hideous are these creatures and so foul their breath that anyone who comes near one is certain to die, their flesh and bones consumed by the horrible creature.

In the seventeenth century, a room in the White Hart which is now the boardroom would double as a court when the Guildhall had large numbers of cases to try. At her trial here, a young woman was sentenced to death on some very inaccurate evidence. It is thought that she still haunts the boardroom, silently protesting her innocence. The inn's courtyard is haunted by an old woman dressed in a black cape, who cries and wrings her hands. Hotel staff believe that she is the mother of the unfortunate condemned woman.

I spoke to the Duty Manager who was keen to tell me about the ghost of an unhappy little boy in old-fashioned clothing who she has often seen crying. Several concerned guests have also seen him, but whenever anyone tries to speak to him he becomes frightened and runs away. No one knows why the child is unhappy, but at the beginning of the twentieth century a landlord lived on the premises with his large family. He was known as a very harsh man whose children were terrified of him.

Across the courtyard are separate rooms which are today used as managers' accommodation. The Duty Manager I spoke to has often seen the ghost of a little girl in a

The White Hart Hotel.

The mysterious well at the White Hart.

long dress sitting on the steps as if waiting for someone. On several occasions she has also been seen by the cleaner when she is sweeping the steps. The courtyard was once used by horse-drawn coaches. The Duty Manager has seen the fleeting image of a man wearing an old-fashioned three-cornered hat and carrying a coachman's whip. In the same area a women in Puritan dress from the Civil War period has been seen walking. At first only the top half of her body is visible. Then her legs and feet appear as if she is climbing unseen steps. Since the Civil War there have been a lot of alterations in the courtyard; today the ground level is different and steps which once led up to maid's accommodation are no longer there.

Hotel receptionists told me that in one of the guest bedrooms there is a priest hole once used for hiding persecuted Catholic priests. A number of guests complained about experiencing unsettled nights. Some claimed to have felt the bed moving. The bed faced the corner where the priest hole was hidden behind a bookcase. Staff rearranged the room so that the bed now faces the other way. Since then there have been no more complaints. Perhaps the ghost of a hidden priest is anxious to remain undiscovered?

A barmaid admitted that she is unhappy about going to the hotel's attic alone. Part of it was burnt out in a fire in the 1800s. Since it has been made safe and is used to store spare furniture and bulk food items. However, it has a dreadfully oppressive atmosphere. Boxes and stacks of goods are often found overturned as if someone has moved them in a hurry. A number of guests in the attic rooms died in the fire. Staff today are convinced that their unfortunate ghosts are still trying to escape unfamiliar smoke-filled rooms.

Motion-activated hand dryers in a disused bathroom next to the attic store go off for no reason. Following investigation an electrician found no evidence of malfunction. Taps have also been found turned on, and although they are firmly turned off, they are later found on again. In the 1980s one of the live-in staff was allowed to keep a dog. When it was taken to the attic it cowered and howled until it was carried out, whereupon it immediately became calm again.

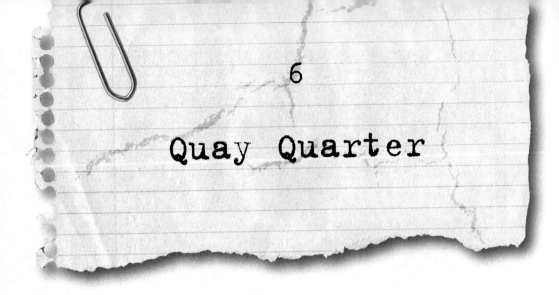

6

Quay Quarter

IN the 1970s Exeter Quay became famous when it appeared in the seafaring drama *The Onedin Line*. Renovations in the 1980s have turned the Quay and canal area into one of the nicest parts of the city and thousands of people enjoy themselves here every year. Today the Quay Quarter is a pleasant haven, but this hasn't always been the case!

The Canal

Exeter Canal was built in the 1560s to enable ships to reach Exeter Quay. In the 1930s a local prostitute named Edith went missing and her strangled body was found floating in the canal. She had been desperate for money and not fussy who she took as clients. Her friends assumed that one of her customers had killed her but police suspected her estranged husband. After extensive investigations no real evidence was found, and no one was ever tried for the crime.

The sound of a woman screaming has been heard by a number of people over the years. Often they have rushed to help, thinking that someone is being assaulted on the canal's dark banks. None of the would-be rescuers has ever found anything and thorough police searches have failed to yield anything to help solve this mystery. Locals believe that the noise is the ghost of poor Edith who, having been killed so violently, is unable to find rest.

The Quay

One misty winter night in 1989 a man named James was walking his dog along the Quay next to the Old Quay House. He had followed this route many times because he enjoyed looking at the tranquil water. Soon, however, he changed his mind!

Out of the mist he could see something strange on the river. In an article in the *Exeter Herald* dated 5 October 1989, James described his experience:

> Suddenly there appeared a blue light having the same intensity as a blow lamp. In the centre of the light there was a long boat with curved ends. About thirty men in animal fleeces manned the oars. In the bow a red bearded man raised his shield in the direction of Exeter and if there had been a sound I am certain it would have been a curse. I have never seen such an expression of hatred before.

Quay House, site of the
Viking ship appearance

The river Exe.

The River Exe.

James' dog began to whine, slipped its collar and ran away. The ship then mysteriously vanished. Later the dog was found cowering behind a stack of building materials outside the Quay House, which was being renovated. James tried to make the dog walk back in the direction from which the longship had appeared. The animal refused and had to be carried howling and quaking in fear.

In another edition of the newspaper dated 19 October an unnamed academic wrote:

> The Danes used to raid along the western coast and penetrate with their ships as far inland as possible. King Sweyn of the Danes developed a deep hatred of Exeter and when his sister was murdered his revenge was to sail up the Exe and burn the city.

For years there has been speculation about the validity of this story. I wondered if James had just been seeking his fifteen minutes of fame, but later he admitted that he had been ridiculed so much that he nearly withdrew his permission for the paper to use his story. Could it have been a student joke? If so, it was very elaborate – and how on earth did the vessel disappear? The debate goes on.

The River Exe

The once run-down quay area used to be anything but safe and there were a number of incidents. A coroners report appeared in the *Exeter Flying Post* on 13 January 1912:

> John Taylor, an eighty year old retired cabinet maker, was out walking at 8 p.m. on the 4 January. It was not usual for him to venture down to the river which is badly lit. It was a foggy night and it may be supposed that Mr Taylor took a wrong turn. He may have stumbled over rough ground at the river's edge. At any event, he fell into the water. His cries alerted security men at a warehouse some way along the bank. It took them some time to find Mr Taylor, but they eventually managed to pull him out using grappling irons. The old man was taken to hospital where he died two hours later. Death was due to a combination of hypothermia and asphyxia due to water in the lungs.

The river bank from which Mr Taylor fell is now part of Piazza Terracina, a well-lit, paved area popular with visitors. Usually it is a peaceful setting, but on January nights strange echoing screams have been heard. The river appears agitated as if someone is splashing, though investigations have proved that no one is in the water.

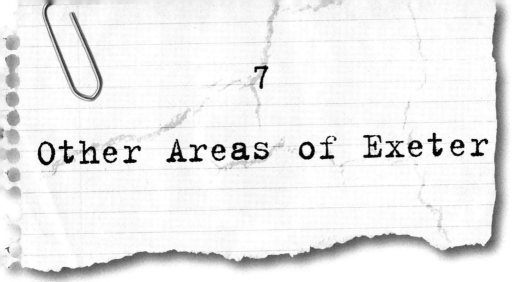

7

Other Areas of Exeter

Heavitree

The name 'Heavitree' is thought to date from the Saxon Period and means 'Gallows Tree'. There were two main sites of execution in the area at different times.

Local writer Heidi Stevenson told me that several years ago, while working in radio, she interviewed the famous paranormalist Uri Geller. He told her that he and his son had visited Heavitree and both felt a strange and disturbing affinity with that part of the city, knowing, without being told, that terrible things had happened there. When I contacted Uri he confirmed the story and kindly gave permission for it to be used in this book.

Heavitree Park

An ethereal African woman in an elaborate headdress has been seen looking at the flowers and shrubs in the park late at night.

Heavitree Pleasure Ground was opened in 1906 near the site of a former workhouse. She is reputedly a freed slave from West Africa who was brought to Exeter, becoming an inmate of the workhouse in the 1850s. She was known for her bright headwear and sunny disposition. It is said that even the austerity of the workhouse was better than her former life in slavery and that her spirit can't leave the place where she was so content.

Livery Dole and Gallow's Cross

For hundreds of years until the 1530s, executions were carried out at Livery Dole, the junction of Heavitree, Polsloe and Magdalen Roads. Executions were a gruesome entertainment for the public; the more notorious the crime, the better. Most murderers were hanged, but the punishment for poisoning, treason and heresy was to be burned at the stake. Before the burning began notorious heretic 'criminals' might have burning twigs pushed into their blasphemous mouths by spectators outraged at their 'crime'.

The execution site stands in a busy area today, but even in daylight the atmosphere is unsettling. I asked local people what they knew of the place and whether they had ever seen anything unusual. Many didn't know the history of Livery Dole, but a number reported seeing strange hovering lights, on the side of the building, though no one had been in the small garden at the time.

A lady by the name of Charlotte told me that on their way home from work one evening, she and her friend had heard muffled screaming coming from Livery Dole Gardens. Thinking that a crowd of youngsters were messing about and that it had got out of hand, the ladies peered in. The noise continued, but no one was there. Charlotte told me, 'I certainly don't hang around there any more, especially now you've told me the horrible things that used to go on!'

Only one person I spoke to knew that there was once a site of execution at Livery Dole and ironically, even though he lived close to the spot, he had never experienced anything remotely spooky there!

When Exeter became a county in its own right in the 1530s, the execution site moved to Gallows Cross, at the junction of Sidmouth and Honiton Roads. Executed bodies were found a few years ago when building work was being carried out nearby. Today a car wash stands near the site of the graves.

In 1782 Rebecca Downing, aged fifteen, was burnt at Gallows Cross after being found guilty of poisoning her employer Richard Jarvis on very flimsy evidence. The execution was covered in the *Flying Post* of 2 August 1782:

> Rebecca Downing was on Monday last pursuant to her sentence, drawn on a fledge to the place of execution, attended by an amazing concourse of people, where after being strangled, her body was burnt to ashes. While under sentence and at the place of her execution she appeared totally ignorant and insensible of her situation.

It is thought that Rebecca suffered from severe learning difficulties and that she didn't understand what she was confessing to. The judge's verdict was not popular among the people of Exeter. Perhaps this is why her story lives on.

The ghost of a young girl dressed in white has been seen walking down the middle of Sidmouth Road late at night. Her arms are out in front of her and she moved in jerks as if being pulled by someone unseen. Concerned motorists who turn their vehicles round to help are disconcerted to see the figure gradually fade from view as they approach.

Sidmouth Road

Late one night in the summer of 1964, a young Marine named Mike was making his way along Sidmouth Road on his way back to barracks. As he passed the police headquarters he heard heavy footsteps behind him. Thinking that it might be another Marine, and that they could share their walk, he slowed down. But as he did the footsteps stopped. Mike looked round and although he had a clear view right down the road, could see no one. He continued walking and the footsteps began again, accompanied by deep noisy breathing as if someone was sobbing. Mike stopped again, but the footsteps and breathing noise got closer. As the sounds passed him Mike felt a sudden icy breeze on the back of his neck, even though the night was warm and windless. Back at the barracks he told the story to his friends imagining, that they would laugh at his overactive imagination. However, two other Marines had also heard strange breathy noises in the same area.

St Loyes Chapel, Hurst Avenue

The tiny ruined chapel of St Loyes was built in the early 1400s and is dedicated to St Loye, a seventh-century French bishop who became the patron saint of metalworkers. Today there are modern houses

Livery Dole execution site.

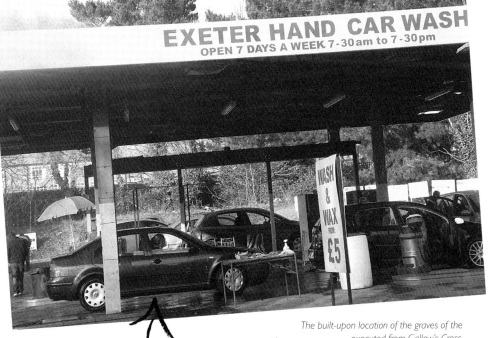

The built-upon location of the graves of the
executed from Gallow's Cross.

St Loyes Chapel.

and a busy road near the chapel. I had heard rumours of strange hovering red lights inside the ruins. These were seen during the 1940s and '50s, but I couldn't help feeling disappointed by its lack of a spooky atmosphere when I first saw it. As I was looking round, a local man, Mr Andrews, stopped for a chat. He had heard of the red lights too and could add to the story.

During the 1980s, Mr Andrews used to walk past the ruined structure soon after dawn on the way to his delivery driver's job. On several occasions he saw large shadowy shapes which made him think of people wearing long cloaks. They passed across a glassless window which would have been on the upper floor. Mr Andrews said that what made him stop to look is the fact that there is no floor left in the upper part of the building. Whatever was up there was standing on thin air. Other locals have also seen the shapes in the window as recently as 2010.

Newtown

Newtown is an area located roughly between Sidwell Street and Heavitree. Until 200 years ago, the area was farmland, but there is evidence of clay mining for the manufacture of bricks in the sixteenth century. Like several other areas of the city, Newtown suffered badly in the bombing of May 1942.

Belmont Road
In 1826 large and very atmospheric houses for the wealthy of Exeter were built near Belmont Park. These proved very popular

Haunted house on Belmont Road.

The staircase at
Belmont Road.

as the area was pleasant and away from the hustle and bustle of the city centre.

Jonathon, the current owner of one of the properties, is a spiritual healer. He invited me into his beautiful home and let me wander about on my own to allow me to gain my own impressions. The basement is a light and airy flat decorated in cheery colours, but its atmosphere wasn't cheery to me. Instead, it felt oppressive and momentarily seemed to grow darker. I was glad to get out!

Later Jonathon told me about the strange experiences he has often had in the house, which he and his family bought in 1996. Soon after, he began to be aware of a presence which made itself felt on the stairs of the first floor and basement. Up to this point the basement had not been mentioned by either of us. As I sat mulling this over, Jonathon told me that sometimes he caught a glimpse of the faint image of a woman in early Victorian dress. His impression was that the woman was not a servant, but was probably the ghost of an early tenant. Although he could not detect any bad atmosphere, none of Jonathon's family were happy in the house alone, especially at night.

Eventually, Jonathon decided to invite some of his friends round from the Spiritualist church in an attempt to encourage the ghost to move on into the next life. Unfortunately this did not work. One evening, Jonathon was sitting in the basement room alone when he decided to try summoning the ghost himself in the hope that he would encourage it to leave. He briefly felt, rather than saw, the presences of several ghosts. Interestingly Jonathon told me that he has only ever actually seen one other spook and that was many years ago, though he can sense them.

Clifton Hill

In 1978 my friend Gordon had just married. He and his wife were pleased to find a nice bedsit at a reasonable rent on Clifton Hill. A few days after they moved in, one of Gordon's wife's slippers disappeared. As the weather had turned cold they began to look for it. Although they lifted the bed, looked in the wardrobe and all the drawers it was not to be found. The bedsit was very small and they were puzzled as to what had happened to the slipper, but soon forgot about it in their preparations for Christmas, which was just a week away.

On Christmas morning they got out of bed and in the middle of the floor was the lost slipper in a spot they had walked over hundreds of times. Gordon told me, 'There is no way we could have missed it and it wasn't my wife playing a joke – she was absolutely terrified by its sudden appearance.'

When Gordon crossed the room to pick it up he suddenly felt icily cold and the air seemed thicker and hard to breathe. As he moved away from the spot it was instantly warmer and the air became normal again. After this occasion, they also noticed a cold spot in one corner. This was where the kitchenette was located and should have been the warmest part of the room. Gordon's wife often felt suddenly very cold even when she was lifting food out of the hot oven. Until this time Gordon felt that the existence of ghosts and poltergeists was nonsense, but the building where his bedsit was located is over 200 years old and events there have changed his mind.

Hanover Road

In the 1990s, a family in Hanover Road complained that they were disturbed on two nights by the appearance of intense bright lights in their bedrooms which hovered over their bodies. As if this wasn't bad enough, the whole family felt something gripping their arms and legs as if trying to stop them moving. This only lasted for a few seconds, but in the mornings their limbs were badly bruised.

Unsurprisingly, the family moved in with relatives soon after and were later rehoused.

St David's

There were farms here 1,000 years ago, but the area didn't really become part of the Exeter until the city expanded in the nineteenth century. This is a spooky area and well worth a visit!

Bonhay Road flats.

Bonhay Road

Bonnie and her partner moved into a new flat on Bonhay Road while looking for a place to buy. From the day they moved in Bonnie could never settle. Given that it was a bright new flat, the atmosphere was inexplicably eerie and she hated to be alone there. Not wanting to worry her partner, she didn't mention her concerns to him until after they had moved out.

To her surprise her partner admitted that he had felt exactly the same. Intrigued, they decided to look into the history of the area to see if any light could be shed on the matter. After some research they found that the block of flats was built on the site of an old inn, the Lazy Landlord, once known as the Princess Alexandra. This had been demolished in 2002. One room of the Lazy Landlord had occasionally been used for laying out dead bodies and this was located exactly where the young couple's flat was.

In 1879, a six-month-old baby named Reginald Hide went missing in the Bonhay area. His body was eventually found in Powhay leat, a nineteenth-century watercourse dug to supply power which ran behind the inn. Horrifyingly, Reginald had

been hacked to bits. His body was one of those laid out in the pub. Eventually local woman Annie Took was hanged for his murder.

The ghost of a little crying boy has been seen by a number of locals on Bonhay Road. He looks both ways along the road as if waiting for someone. John, who lives nearby and has seen the boy twice, told me that it was his old-fashioned clothing that he noticed first. When John approached to see if he could help, the boy vanished. The first time this happened he assumed that the lad had merely gone through a door, and thought no more of it. The second time he saw the crying boy, the lad disappeared through a brick wall!

On John's side of the road the houses date from the Victorian period and John believes that the sad boy lived in Bonhay Road, but who he was and what happened to him remains a mystery.

Bury Meadow.

Bury Meadow

Bury Meadow actually got its name from a previous owner of the land, a 'Mr Berry'. As we shall see, the change of pronunciation is morbidly appropriate! Many visitors today have no idea about the grisly past of Bury Meadow, which is now a pleasant park – during daylight hours, at least.

In 1832, Exeter was hit by an outbreak of cholera. Several hundred people died, mostly from the poorer areas of the city where overcrowding and lack of clean water ensured that the disease took hold. Most people afflicted by cholera died horribly.

Bury Meadow was allocated as a graveyard. Cholera victims were interred quickly in the dark in an attempt to avoid panic among the city's population. Rumours were rife that some of those buried were

not even dead. There was little ceremony in the proceedings and materials for the burials were collected hurriedly. When the last cholera victim was buried, the grave digger temporarily laid a very old gravestone on top of the new grave. The stone bore the name Salathiel Jennings, who died in 1637. Locals claimed to see Salathiel, rising from her grave, searching for her grave stone. Only after the stone was replaced did she rest peacefully again.

In recent times, strange noises have been heard in the park at night. Creaking and rattling like the sound of wooden wheels is accompanied by loud sobbing and scraping. The noise stops if anyone goes to investigate.

I sat in Bury Meadow Park late one night with my partner, Seal. There were no unexplained noises, but the atmosphere was dreadful, in spite of the nearby street lights and our powerful torches. We were very glad to leave.

Elm Grove Road

Elm Grove Road, a row of lovely Georgian houses, runs along the back of Bury Meadow. In 2007 Kelli Melson, a student at the time, was renting a flat there. Kelli was always rushing out to lectures or to her part-ime job, and was careful with her keys. She made a point of always leaving them on a tray in her bedroom. Every day the keys had moved, even though she was living in the flat alone. Kelli would find them under her pillow, in the corner of the room or on the window sill. One morning she was running late and, as usual, her keys were not in their tray. In exasperation Kelli exclaimed, 'I don't have time for this right now!' The keys suddenly appeared from under the bed sliding across the carpet. Far from being frightened by these events, Kelli generally found them amusing and told me, 'It was as if a little child was playing a mischievous trick'. I asked Kelli if she had heard the story of Bury Meadow. She hadn't, but told me, 'My room looked right over the park, if I'd known it was once a graveyard, and is now haunted, I would have felt less happy about the strange situation with my keys!'

The Imperial Hotel, North Road

The Imperial Hotel, constructed in 1810 features a huge semi-circular metal and glass wall copied from a design by Isambard Kingdom Brunel. It became a hotel in 1923 and was renamed The Imperial Public House in 1996. The building was derelict for several years before being turned into a pub and because of its valuable architectural fixtures and fittings, it was guarded by a private security firm.

One of their guards, Jim, had a number of scary experiences on the site. One morning at about 1 a.m. he was undertaking a patrol inside the building near the kitchens when he suddenly heard a man's voice close to his ear. Jim did a thorough search but found nothing. He mentioned it to his colleague, who said that he had had a similar experience in the same place but had dismissed it as his imagination. At the time, the guards had their own hut outside the front entrance, but this was removed when the grounds were being landscaped. Instead they were given a small room near the kitchens. Although the heating was kept on at night to avoid damp, Jim and the other guard often experienced a sudden extreme drop in temperature. This continued when the heating was turned off for the summer, which that year was very warm. Jim and his colleague vacated their room for good when, at different times, they felt a chilly tapping sensation as if someone was running cold fingers down their backs while they were sitting in one particular old chair.

The Imperial Hotel kitchen entrance.

The University of Exeter, Streatham Campus

The University of Exeter was formed in 1955 when a Royal Charter amalgamated the University Colleges of the South West. Many of its imposing buildings predate the university by many years and there are numerous ghost stories about them.

Queen's Building

In 1998 there were reports of the late-night appearance of a strange, pale man near the Queen's Building. A number of students approached the man wondering what he wanted. One noticed that he had livid marks on his neck. On being addressed the man said nothing, but pointed to a large and very old tree nearby. Then he pointed at his neck before hurrying round the corner of the building, followed by the students. To their amazement the man vanished. The tree he indicated is a Judas tree, said to be of the type from which Judas Iscariot hanged himself after betraying Christ. In previous centuries the wood from such trees was used to construct gallows and the trees themselves were sometimes used for impromptu executions.

Thomas Hall

In the late 1600s Thomas Hall was called Great Duryard House. Tragically, the daughter of its owner met her death at the age of thirteen when she fell down the cellar steps, hitting her head. Her father, Sir Thomas Jeffers, was distraught and had the cellar bricked up so that he never again had to look at the place where his daughter died.

Although there is no way into the cellar today, footsteps have been heard on the steps by many people. When the university took over the building a garden was planted. This should be a pleasant place for students to take breaks, but I found it to have a very unpleasant atmosphere and most people don't seem to linger for long.

The Washington Singer Building

The imposing Washington Singer Building near the entrance of the campus was built by a philanthropist of the same name in 1931. Today it houses the Psychology Faculty.

A former university porter, George, recalls an event which took place during one of his all-night security shifts in the late 1990s. The Washington Singer Building contained a lot of valuable computer equipment and was checked several times each night. George recalled, 'As I entered the computer room I heard a noise behind me. I thought it was strange because I hadn't heard the corridor doors swing shut. Expecting to see a student I went into the corridor and saw a young man.'

George tried to explain that the building was shut until 8 a.m., but the youth stayed silent. Turning to a shelf the porter picked up a leaflet listing opening times, but when he turned round the young man had gone.

The doors at the end of the corridor leading to other floors were all locked and there was no explanation as to how the young man had disappeared so quickly. 'I thought some of the lads were playing a prank and it made me chuckle,' George said. 'But I was responsible for the building, so I went to check all the doors. Every one, including the front entrance was locked'.

Returning to the porter's lodge he looked in the key cupboard. The only spare set of keys was still there. Not until later did George realise that the man he had seen was wearing old-fashioned clothing, 'like something you see in pictures from before the Second World War'.

A painter and decorator is said to haunt parts of the university. He has been seen university flat late one night in the 1960s. She was annoyed to be woken suddenly by a grating noise followed by a loud thudding. Students will be students, and the lady hurried to the door meaning to give them a piece of her mind for getting up to silly pranks at such a late hour. What she saw must have affected her sleep for many nights to come. On the ground outside her home stood a pale monk struggling to push a heavy barrow up the sloping grass. Still believing that it was some sort of student jape, the lady didn't realise what was in the barrow at first. Then she looked and saw the naked and badly bleeding corpse of a woman. The lady screamed and the apparition suddenly vanished.

St James

St James Park, the home ground of Exeter City Football club, is located in this area of Exeter to the north of the city centre. St James is a mixture of buildings ranging from the 1800s to the modern period.

Pennsylvania Road

In 1999 Michael Evans, former General Secretary of the Exeter Spiritualist Church, was called out to a house in Pennsylvania Road. This belonged to a doctor and her fiancé who were spending all their spare time renovating the building. Her fiancé had had a terrible fright when he opened a cupboard and saw two bloody arms bound by a rope. The young man hastily slammed the cupboard shut. He then reopened it. Although the apparition had gone, he was so frightened that he fled the house, refusing to spend any time in it alone.

Michael and his team spent an evening in the house in the room where the cupboard was located. Michael's colleague,

The Washington Singer building at the University of Exeter.

several times by students and lecturers since the 1960s carrying a ladder and paint pots around the grounds. What makes him noticeable is that he is only ever seen at night, long after the maintenance staff have finished their work for the day. Presumably he used to be employed by the university or in one of the large formerly private houses which now form part of the campus. No one knows who he was or why he is still haunts his former place of work.

The wife of a lecturer told the following story to her friend Miss French and later it appeared in the 'Report and Transactions of the Devonshire Association for the Advancement of Science, Literature and the Arts', 1980. The lady was asleep in their

Ron, a medium, contacted the spirit of a man in the room.

Ron asked, 'What is your name?'

The spirit replied 'Jacob'. He then added 'I do not know where I am now, but I have recollection of another place, a horrible place.'

Ron asked, 'Where was that?'

To which Jacob replied, 'A place of execution. Rope around my neck.'

Ron inquired, 'And what did you do?'

Jacob became agitated and said, 'I stole a horse.'

Michael joined the conversation, asking, 'What year was this? Who was on the throne?'

Jacob replied, 'It was in the reign of Queen Victoria.' Then he said, 'All I can really try to explain to you is that I want to get away from where I am.'

Michael assured him, 'We can help you do that. Look upwards. What do you see?'

Jacob replied, 'I see my dead brother.'

Ron asked the spirit, 'Will you go with him?'

Jacob replied, 'I will go most happily with him, but I must apologise to the man I frightened in this place.'

Michael told the spirit, 'We will let him know that.'

After this event the doctor and her fiancé experienced no further spiritual disturbances in their home.

St Loyes

St Loyes has a lovely rural feel thanks to its proximity to Ludwell Valley Park. Here it is possible to enjoy tranquil farmland and stunning views, but the area hasn't always been so peaceful!

The Friendly Ghost

In 1795 late one night a young man was returning to his family in Exeter after spending some time abroad. As he rode through farmland at St Loyes, on the outskirts of the city, he was surprised to see Madam Gould, the local landowner's wife. She was dressed in white and standing in a field looking up at the stars. The young man wished her good evening and waved. She smiled and waved back. Madam Gould was known to be fond of walking in the countryside, but the young man was puzzled as to why she should be out so late. When he told his family what he had seen they were very shocked. Madam Gould had been buried for a week.

Today some of this land is built on. What remains is always dark and gloomy, even in sunny weather. Local people still know the area as 'White Lady Field'. In 1997 a group of tourists camped there one night, not knowing the story. They were woken up in the small hours by someone shaking the tent. On looking out they saw a dim white figure running across the field.

The Murder Field

In the 1970s, Miss Higgins was in the habit of early morning walks. One day she decided to collect some wild mushrooms from a field near her home to enjoy with her breakfast as she had often done before, being an expert on fungi and other edible wild plants. Concerned friends tried to stop her as they had heard that the particular field that Miss Higgins planned to visit was haunted.

'I rejected this as superstitious mumbo jumbo,' the level-headed Miss Higgins told the *Exeter Herald* in an interview on 19 October 1989.

After enjoying her walk, Miss Higgins went home for her well-earned breakfast.

She carefully washed the mushrooms, then fried them with bacon. As she enjoyed her meal, Miss Higgins smiled to herself about her misguided friends' fear of ghosts. She has no explanation for what happened next. 'Suddenly I became aware of a strange presence,' Miss Higgins said. 'A tall female figure stood behind me mouthing the words "pick axe" over and over. As quickly as she appeared, she vanished.'

Later Miss Higgins decided to look into the history of the area she had been walking in and an elderly local told her that in 1909 a young man had killed his girlfriend, who had ended their relationship, in that very field.

St Thomas

In the south west of the city, St Thomas was once an important part Exeter's trade route. An abundance of fertile farmland land meant that much of the area once belonged to a religious order. Today this gives ghost hunters a lot to go on, as you will see!

Bowhill House, Dunsford Road

Bowhill House on Dunsford Road was built around 1450. The building became the St Thomas Hospital for Lunatics in the early 1800s and continued as such until the 1860s.

Today this rather striking building is used as business premises by a number of local firms. Chris from a company of architects kindly showed me round. The upper floors had a mellow atmosphere and none of the people working there today had ever felt anything strange. The ground floor was different. The kitchen and largest room downstairs were brooding with a heavy atmosphere and I actually felt quite disturbed. Later I discovered that this large room had been where doctors had once carried out their barbaric 'treatments' such as long ice-cold baths and purging.

For many years, people have reported banging noises and anguished howls coming from the building late at night and I had heard that a number of suicides had taken place while Bowhill House was an asylum. One of Chris' colleagues told me that in 1820 an unfortunate patient set fire to herself and jumped out of a window.

Later I was taking photographs of the outside of Bowhill House when a Mrs Earnshaw stopped to watch. She told me that she has seen the shadowy figure of a woman in a long dress lying on the ground in Bowhill's courtyard. On returning minutes later with a torch she found that the figure had gone. Other people in the area told her that they have seen strange lights in the grounds rising to above roof level before disappearing.

Cowick Barton Inn, Cowick Lane

The name 'Cowick' comes from a Saxon village name 'Coic'. The Parish of Cowick is mentioned in the Domesday Book of 1086. From the 1100s to the 1500s the land belonged to Cowick Priory before being given to Sir John Tyrell. He converted the priory into a fine house in the 1540s. Since 1963 this building has been the Cowick Barton Inn, and must rate as one of the most haunted places in the city.

Owners Keely and Steve have organised several psychic nights at the inn. At one, a medium, Julie, said she could see men in long robes warming themselves by the fire, which is an original feature of the building. At another event a medium by the name of John was able to draw the ghosts he could see. One was definitely a monk, but another picture showed a man with tools which was a puzzle at first. Then Keely discovered that there had been a blacksmith's forge on the premises.

On 10 May 2010 I organised an investigation at the Cowick Barton Inn along with paranormalist Tony Eccles, sound engineer Lee Rawlings and my partner Seal Faulkner, up to this point still a non-believer in ghosts. The following section of this book is made up of Keely and Steve's experiences and those of other visitors combined with the results of our investigation.

The Bar

A couple at the bar were recently choosing meals from the menu with the help of a barman. The order, including table number, was sent to the kitchen as usual. The waiter took the food to the correct table only to be told by the people sitting there that they hadn't ordered any. Cross at having food wasted, the chef checked the security camera. It showed the barman writing an order. He appeared to be talking, but no one was there. When asked, he had no recollection of taking any food orders at the time.

Keely took me behind the bar to show me a metal bell which was previously used to alert waiting staff that food was ready. On several nights, the bell has fallen violently from its shelf as if someone had dropped it. A barman who picked it up found that it was so hot that it burned his hand. When I looked at the shelf where the bell is kept, I could see that there is no way it could have fallen by itself.

Customers at one particular table in the bar have seen strange hovering shadows on the nearby wall though no one is near enough to make them. Above this table, a clock standing on a shelf would suddenly fly off and land across the room. Eventually the clock broke and was replaced by a heavy framed picture. When this took flight, Steve removed it in case someone was hit. Now the shelf is empty.

There is an unexplained cold spot behind the bar. Staff need only move a few inches and the temperature is much warmer. We were invited to stand on the cold spot. The difference in temperature from the rest of the bar area is very noticeable and very, very creepy!

The Restaurant

In 2009, a couple who were eating in the restaurant saw a figure walk across the room and pass right through the wall. A ghost in long robes has also been seen in this room looking at the layout of the tables.

Steve told me that in the restaurant he often sees figures out of the corner of his eye. The most common of these is a figure dressed in white robes. When he turns to look there is nothing there.

Our investigation team set up our recording equipment in the restaurant after all the customers had left. Disappointingly the disk was empty of sound. As we were packing Lee and an astonished Seal simultaneously saw a strange white light hovering a foot or so above the floor before seeming to disappear through the wall.

The Ladies' Toilets

Keely told me that the toilet room suddenly becomes very cold for no reason and the atmosphere grows heavy. Then the temperature rises again just as quickly. The heating system has been checked but there are no problems with it.

The Monk's Room

This is quite a small room which is mainly used for storage. On the window sill is a framed Bible reference from Phil 3v14

Bowhill House.

Bowhill House ground floor.

The bar at the Cowick Barton Inn.

The Cowick Barton Inn restaurant.

which reads 'I press towards the mark for the prize of the high calling of God in Christ Jesus'. This is said to refer to the mechanism for opening a secret priest's hole which may have been in the cellar beneath the Monk's Room. Unfortunately the cellar is now bricked up. On the wall of the Monk's Room is an ancient plaster plaque which also features the Bible reference number.

Coded Bible reference in the Monk's Room at the Cowick Barton Inn.

The corridor between the bar and the Monk's Room also goes cold very suddenly, though there is no window or external door to allow a draught in.

Misty, the owners' dog, hates the Monk's Room. She often snarls and growls at the doorway though nothing seems to be there. Just inside this door the chef has seen a shadowy figure in long robes. One night when the inn was shut Keely could hear a scraping noise coming from the Monk's Room. No one was there, but a table had been moved leaving marks on the floor.

When the last customer had left and the building was quiet, Lee set up his recording equipment in the Monk's Room. When we played it back not only were there shuffling noises, but also something sounding like breathing.

Accompanied by Keely's sister Callie, we again set up our recording equipment in the Monk's Room. This time Tony, who is an expert in Electric Voice Phenomenon (EVP) recordings, suggested that we should ask questions of any spirits in the room. Our questions and the sounds picked up are as follows.

Tony welcomed any spirits and asked them to answer us. He then asked the spirits, 'Are you happy?' On listening to the recording later a faint noise like a woman's voice was detected.

Lee asked, 'What is your name?' Again there was a faint voice.

Callie asked, 'How old were you when you died? When did you die?' This time there was a louder, child-like scream.

Our group sat staring at each other in disbelief across the table. Seal suddenly left the room and refused to go back in.

Staff Accommodation
The little daughter of the Karen's friend was heard talking in one of the inn's bedrooms. When her mother looked into the room there was no one there. Thinking that the child was just playing, her mother thought nothing of it until the little girl asked who the man in the corner with the 'sticky out lace collar and funny baggy trousers' was. A few days later there was a programme about Tudor history on TV and the little girl said the man she had been talking to was dressed just like the people in the programme.

When she was trying to sleep in another bedroom Callie heard shuffling footsteps cross the room. The next day she left her camcorder running while the inn was empty. Listening to it later, she heard noises like drawers being open and shut as if someone was looking for something. Unfortunately, when Lee left his more sophisticated recording equipment running in this particular room, it picked nothing up.

The Attics

When engineers were in the attic rewiring the smoke and burglar alarms one of them was horrified to see the figure of a monk watching him from the corner. When the man looked again, the monk had gone. The man refused to work up there by himself again.

A few days later, the same workmen found a collection of old bones under the loft floorboards. The wooden floors are original and quite probably had not been lifted for hundreds of years. When the bones were tested they proved to be from a goat, a sheep and a horse. Perhaps not as grisly as finding human bones, but why had someone hidden them in the loft?

In the middle of the night, frantic bounding footsteps can often be heard crossing the wooden floor of the attic. The first time this happened the inn's owners thought that Misty might have found her way up the attic stairs, but the attic was empty and the dog was found sleeping peacefully in her basket.

A number of customers have reported seeing the sad face of a young man peering through a tiny window in the attic gable when no one has been up there. This area of the loft is now partitioned off and contains electric boxes and the TV aerial. No one, not even Keely (who is unfazed by apparent hauntings), will go up there alone as the atmosphere is horrible. I steeled myself to look through the hatch, but saw and felt nothing.

Outside the Cowick Barton Inn

A lady in a long velvet dress has been seen outside the main building. She appears to be looking for something and is distressed. If anyone tries to speak to her, she disappears through the wall at a point where an ancient door has been filled in.

While Lee was talking to a couple of the inn's regulars outside the main entrance he saw a shadowy figure disappear round the corner. He later told me that the man he was talking to said, 'You saw it too?' Unknown to Lee at the time, a ghostly shadow has been seen many times in the same spot.

In the 1500s, several women were assaulted in the area. One night a scream was heard and a young man who was making cheese ran to investigate, taking with him the cheese wire he had been using. He saw a figure attacking a young girl and realised it was his sister. In a rage, the young man garrotted the attacker with such force that he was decapitated. The dead man was found to be a monk. Though the body was later removed, its head was never found. In modern times, locals claim to have seen a ghostly man dragging a headless corpse.

For many years, the location of the priory graveyard was lost. Then, in the 1880s, several ancient bodies were unearthed in the field behind the inn. One was buried in a stone coffin which can now be seen in St Nicholas Priory in the city. The bodies were all removed for reburial and today it is difficult to see where they had been. Luckily I discovered a 1907 map showing the location of the graveyard in the Devon Record Office. From measurements I took it is obvious that the graves were within 20m of the side of the inn. A local woman, Kelly, told me that both she and her mother have seen the ghostly monks here.

Other locals have often seen the ghostly figures of monks too. Mrs Hayman and Mrs Jenkins of nearby Wellington Road told the *Exeter Express* that the monk had appeared in their bedroom.

In August 1984 Mr Frank Edwards, who lived near the Cowick Barton Inn, gave the following information to the

Gable window at the
Cowick Barton Inn.

Exeter Weekly News. The monks at Cowick Barton belonged to a strict silent order, but one enjoyed chatting up local girls! As a penance to stop him thinking of the pleasures of the flesh, he was forced to lie on an uncomfortable cobbled path. Mr Edwards remembered that as a child in the 1940s he saw the path dug up during some drainage work. It was after this that people began seeing the ghosts.

As we finally left the building in the early hours accompanied by the owners, leaving the inn empty, I looked up at the gable window and saw an odd flicker of movement. At the time I shrugged it off as I wasn't wearing my glasses and the light above the door immediately below the window was a bit dim. On the drive home though, Seal told me that he thought had seen a pale face peering from the gable. He is no longer a paranormal sceptic!

Cowick Street

Cowick Street is in the north of St Thomas. Late at night, ghostly running feet and wails of anguish have been heard on Cowick Street, when no one is about. There was a debtor's prison on the street in the 1800s. Today the site is occupied by Cowick Street Motors, but the arched entrance-way to the prison can still be seen. On the opposite side of the street was the Bridewell Correctional Institution for Women – named after a similar prison in London.

In those days, conditions for most prisoners were notoriously bad and the two establishments on Cowick Street were amongst the worst. Only inmates with money or outside help from friends were able to eat properly. Disease was rife in the damp, overcrowded cells and only people who could find no other employment would work at either prison. Inmates were

Cowick Street debtor's prison entrance.

left at the mercy of guards who were, for the most part, violent drunks.

Over the years so little money was spent on maintaining the Cowick Street prisons that their security was compromised and there were a number of successful escapes. Are the running feet on Cowick Street the sounds of escaping prisoners? And do the tormented cries come from prisoners who were recaptured?

Whipton

Whipton is in the north east of Exeter. Its name comes from 'Wippa', an owner of the land in the Saxon age. Whipton, like other areas, became part of Exeter as the city expanded and its ghost stories range from the ancient to the modern.

The Dead Traveller

The Reverend Sabine Baring Gould was born in Exeter. Today he is best known as the writer of hymns such as 'Onward Christian Soldiers' and as a collector of traditional songs. He was also the author of several books about folklore and ghost stories. As an Anglican priest Baring Gould's work has always been trusted for its accuracy.

One evening in 1919, Baring Gould took a coach across Exeter to Whipton to visit a friend, the Revd Archer. At one of the stops a large red-faced man got in. Although not known to Baring Gould, he proceeded to tell him his life story including what a kind husband and father he was and how, as a butcher, he was generous to poor customers. At his destination, Baring Gould was met by his friend who suddenly began to quake on seeing the red-faced man climb down from the coach. Hurrying Baring Gould away, Archer explained that he had buried the man the week before. He had been a cruel husband and father and had, in fact, been prosecuted for cheating his customers and threatening poor people who owed him money. The man's wife, a gypsy, had put a curse on her husband at his funeral – he would never lie at peace, but would wander afoot forever. There were several sightings of the man over the next few years.

The Roundhead Field

In 1951, a farmer was working in one of his large fields at the edge of Whipton. The field was said to be haunted and the farmer's wife was concerned about him working alone in such a place. Her husband, however, was a practical man without much imagination and he laughed off her concerns and continued his work.

When it began to get dark, the farmer packed up his tools and made his way to the gate at the end of the field to go home. He was puzzled to see that where he expected to find a gate there was only a high thick hedge. Feeling foolish at losing his bearings on his own land the farmer chuckled to himself as he set off in the other direction. But when he got to the other end of the field, he again found only a high hedge. It was winter and the night was cooling rapidly. Fighting off the unease he felt, the farmer decided to walk all the way round the field's perimeter until he found his way out. To keep his spirits up he imagined his wife's laughter when he finally told his tale over a good dinner in their warm farmhouse kitchen.

After trudging right round the field, the farmer still had not found the gate. Believing that he had somehow overlooked it, he pulled dead branches from the hedge and piled them up so he couldn't miss them and then set off in the other direction. When he again came to the pile of branches he began to panic.

Just then he saw lights approaching. Believing that it was some of his labourers come to look for him, he started to wave and shout. As the lights drew nearer, the farmer was stunned to see several men in Civil War Roundhead uniforms swinging their torches as if looking for something. Not seeing or hearing the farmer, they marched right past and suddenly disappeared.

Badly shaken, the farmer was relieved to see more lights. This time they were carried by his workers, who were coming through the gate (which had miraculously reappeared). Some time later, on a market day, the farmer was relating his story to an acquaintance he happened to meet. The man, a keen local historian, told the farmer that Roundhead soldiers had searched for runaway prisoners in that very field.

Summer Lane

There is regularly heavy traffic along Summer Lane, especially at rush hour. The lane runs under the railway line and the bridge has a pedestrian tunnel alongside it for the safety of those on foot. According to a number of locals, its safety is questionable!

In the 1970s, a young man named George was walking home from his girl-friend's house late one night. His route took him through the pedestrian tunnel, but on this occasion something was awry. He retold the story for me:

'I was young, very fit and had just left the army. I didn't scare easily. But for some reason I suddenly experienced a terrible feeling of dread, becoming literally frozen with fear.'

George eventually managed to run. As soon as he came out of the tunnel he began

Summer Lane pedestrian tunnel.

to feel better. He told me that to this day he will take a longer detour rather than go through that tunnel.

May, a shop manager, recalled using the pedestrian tunnel on her way to her new job in 1991. On the first occasion she heard footsteps behind her. As it was the time of day when lots of locals were about she wasn't worried, until she paused to fasten her coat zip and the footsteps also stopped. Beginning to walk faster, May glanced over her shoulder. Though the footsteps were nearer and louder, no one was there. After a busy day at work she forgot the incident.

On another occasion in summer she and a colleague were walking towards the tunnel on their way home. As they got nearer, they could hear a noise like a child screaming. They hurried in, but no one was there. Instead the tunnel suddenly became very cold, though there was no wind to blow through it.

Another local, Andrew, refuses to use the tunnel after an experience he had in 2000. Hearing banging and groaning noises as if someone was being beaten up, Andrew turned to see what was going on and saw the hazy figure of a man. The wall behind was visible through his shimmering body. The man raised his arm as if to throw something. A few seconds later there was a clattering sound behind Andrew as if a stick or other wooden object had hit the ground, though there was nothing there.

When I visited Summer Lane to take photographs, I was surprised that the tunnel was shorter than I'd imagined it would be and the inside looked as if it had been recently painted. As I walked along it though, it felt really strange. I tried to work out if it would feel as creepy if I hadn't already heard the stories and I reckon it would. No one can offer an explanation as to who or what is haunting Summer Lane tunnel.

Wonford

In ancient times, Wonford was a royal hunting ground, though most buildings today date from the Victorian period and later – as do the area's ghost stories.

Burnthouse Lane

An Exeter builder was working late on a church in the Burnthouse Lane area in 1998. The following story about his experiences appeared in the 'Report and Transactions of the Devonshire Association for the Advancement of Science, Literature and the Arts' in 2007.

One evening, while he was working alone, the organ suddenly began to play a funeral dirge. The builder went to investigate because no one was allowed into the church during the repairs for health and safety reasons. As the man approached the organ it fell silent and he heard the church door bang shut as if someone had left. Shrugging, the builder went back to his work. A few minutes later, the music began again and the exasperated man downed tools meaning to give the intruder a piece of his mind. This time the organ music continued, becoming wilder and wilder. The man became aware that the air had become suddenly much colder. When he got near to the organ he was horrified to see that no one was playing it. The music stopped. Rooted to the spot, the builder heard unseen footsteps approaching him down the church aisle. Coming to his senses, he fled and refused to return to finish his job.

Dryden Road

In the 1980s, a woman from Dryden Road complained that the ghostly figure of an undertaker in Victorian clothing had tried to pull her out of bed by her ankles on numerous occasions. So terrified was the unfortunate woman that she left her rented home and moved in with relatives. Her story was featured briefly in the *Exeter Herald* on Thursday 7 September 1989.

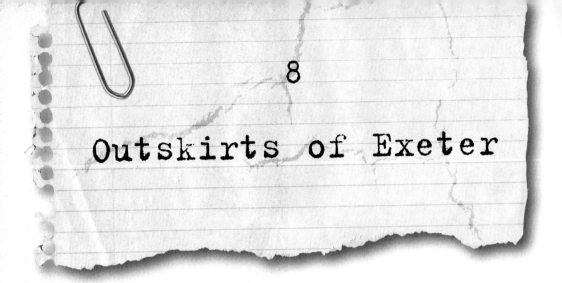

8

Outskirts of Exeter

Exminster

Exminster is a village on the southern edge of Exeter. It became a popular location in the nineteenth century as it was close to Exeter, but retained its countryside appeal. There were a number of fine house built for Exeter's wealthy families in the area.

Kenbury House

During the Victorian period, a most persistent and very unpleasant ghost haunted Kenbury House. There were many complaints from farm workers passing the house at dusk on their way home and from early-morning delivery boys going about their business. Some refused to go near Kenbury House again after seeing a pale ghostly shape hovering over the large ornamental pond. The ghost would screech and moan and clutch at its neck while rolling its hideously piercing red eyes. Several well-meaning parsons tried their best to get rid of the spook by saying prayers or conducting hymn singing by the pond – in the safety of daylight, of course! Unfortunately, the religious ceremonies only made things worse; the apparition became louder and began to appear more often.

Something clearly had to be done. It was decided that several vicars from various parts of Exeter should combine their efforts. One dark night, the clergymen assembled by the pond and conducted an exorcism. The ghost rose from the water screeching horribly before materialising into the shape of a man with a noose around his neck. Undaunted, the vicars continued their solemn prayers and threw holy water at the spectre. It began to moan loudly, twisting as if in agony before plunging back into the pond; it was never seen again. This story appeared in the 'Report and Transactions of the Devonshire Association for the Advancement of Science, Literature and the Arts', in 1973.

Ide

Ide nestles in farmland separated from Exeter by the A30. There are some lovely cottages here – many over 400 years old. Still, picturesque Ide also has some strange tales to tell!

The Haunted Harvest

In the 1930s, a farmer from Ide lost his son at harvest time. The young man had led a rebellious life and was often in trouble. It was said that his unexpected death was due to a combination of drink and an overdose of opium. During the harvest the year after the young man's death, a flame was seen by a farm labourer in one of the corn fields at night. Thinking that some of the dried corn had caught fire, the labourer roused his fellow workers who hurried to douse the fire. Strangely, every time water was thrown over the flame it appeared somewhere else in the field. This continued until daybreak, when the fire suddenly disappeared. Even more strangely, no damage had been done to the corn. It had been the farmer's son's job to check the labourer's work every evening and at dusk he would move around the field making sure that the cut corn was tied correctly.

The Twisted Oak of Ide.

The Twisted Tree

In Ide stands a huge oak with a strangely twisted, corkscrew-like trunk which is hundreds of years old. The trapped spirit of James Pitman is said to haunt the tree and to have caused the peculiar twist in the trunk in his efforts to escape. Pitman hanged himself there in the 1850s, but rumour suggests that he was, in fact, murdered by business rivals. Following Pitman's demise, several mishaps befell the village. Milk turned sour as soon as it came from the cow and no one could get their bread to rise. Worse still, all the beer in the local pub went off! These events were blamed on Pitman's unsettled spirit. In more superstitious times before the First World War, local children were taught to raise their hats respectfully whenever they passed the tree in an attempt to keep the spirit quiet and stop it trying to escape.

Over the years, there have been reports of muffled cries and sounds of a struggle coming from the road near the tree. But no one has ever seen anything when they have investigated.

When I visited Ide I stopped at the Post Office and General Stores to ask for directions to the tree. The lady I spoke to told me that older people in the village who were brought up with the story still refuse to walk past the twisted tree alone at night. The oak stands at the junction of two quiet roads creepily overshadowed by other trees. When I saw 'the Twisted Oak' I could understand the villager's reluctance; although the young barman at the nearby, appropriately named Twisted Oak Pub, told me that he had never seen or heard anything strange.

Kenford

The area of Kenford near Exminster is known as 'Happy Valley', which isn't surprising given the abundance of wonderful thatched houses and attractive open farmland. In spite of this, if you travel alone in the area at night, be prepared to be spooked!

The Ghosts of Tudor Boys

This story appeared in 'Devon and Cornwall Notes and Queries', 1962-64. Late one night, a man approaching Kenford from the south was unsettled to see small boys playing by the side of the road. Worried that they were alone in the dark in a dangerous spot, the man turned his car round intending to help them. As he approached he could see the children in his car headlights and realised that they were wearing odd clothing like that from the Tudor period. As he got closer the children vanished.

At first I was inclined to think that the driver had been in a pub for too long, but villagers in Kenford told me that over the years, since the 1960s, several people have seen strangely dressed children on the road to the south of the village.

Kenton

Kenton Village is about five miles south of Exeter, but is on a regular bus route from Exeter. The village is included because of the fantastically haunted Powderham Castle which is located here.

Powderham Castle

The original castle was built in the 1300s to guard the Exe Estuary and has been owned by the Earls of Devon ever since. I was kindly given an extended private tour of the castle by Peter Dawkes, the senior guide who has been working for the estate for many years. He told me that Powderham has more than its fair share of ghosts!

Perhaps the most famous of Powderham's ghosts is the Grey Lady. She has been seen on numerous occasions both inside the building and outside wandering in the castle grounds. However, no one is certain who the Grey Lady was. Several people who have seen the ghost think that she was Lady Francis who lived in the castle in the eighteenth century. Others, including Peter Dawkes, are convinced that she was a woman who worked for the second Viscount as nanny to his fourteen children in the same period.

Whoever she was, she is a benign ghost who seems to have the family's interests at heart because, since the 1800s, whenever one of the children is ill she has been seen heading towards the church with her head bowed in prayer.

The castle's haunted landing is part of the guided tour. On the wall is a picture of the nanny. For all her kindly behaviour, she looks very severe. Peter walked me backwards and forwards in front of the picture and her terrible stare seemed to follow us wherever we stood!

The Grey Lady often frequents this part of the house. In 2001 a guide-dog refused to cross the landing and barked so furiously at one corner that its owner had to leave. Once away from the landing, the dog reverted to its normal impeccable behaviour. The present Earl's dog, usually an obedient family pet, will not go onto the haunted landing and struggles to get away when brought anywhere near.

In the same corner a hazy grey figure was seen standing behind a visitor in 2009. The man's wife ran from the landing and refused to return. Some of the guides who

Powderham Castle.

been screwed open for twenty-five years after they had mysteriously kept opening on their own, frightening the maids. Lady Devon was not a person to listen to silly stories and refused to believe this explanation – until the carpenter showed her that the screws in the shutters were rusted in solidly.

Over the years many professional photographers have successfully taken pictures of the interior of the castle. On many occasions previously functioning photographic equipment has failed, but only when used on the haunted landing. The last time this happened was when photographs were being taken for the current guidebook in 2006. The photographer moved to another room and his equipment worked perfectly again.

Two hundred years ago, while carrying out repairs to the floor, workmen discovered a boarded-up staircase leading to a hidden room. On ripping the floorboards out the men were horrified to find the skeletons of a woman and baby. They are now buried in the churchyard, but to this day no one knows their identity.

have not seen the Grey Lady themselves can sense her presence. The temperature on the landing often drops rapidly even in warm summer weather.

At the start of the Second World War, the present Earl's late mother was keen that the castle should observe wartime blackout regulations. Lady Devon insisted that she should help hang blackout curtains around the castle.

After carefully putting them up on the window of the 'haunted landing', Lady Devon closed the shutters and went out to check that no light showed. The next night when she went to close the shutters again she was cross to find that someone had screwed them open against the wall. When she asked who had done this, the estate carpenter informed her that they had, in fact,

The castle nursery was built in the Victorian period. Helen Dawkes, wife of Peter, the head guide, works in the castle gift shop. Several times staff have told her that they have heard children's voices in the nursery although no children play there today. When the noises are investigated, the voices stop as soon as anyone enters the room.

One of the castle's long-serving staff has seen a dog in one of the bedrooms. Nothing surprising there, you might think. But the dog has been dead for twenty-five years!

Mysterious window on the haunted landing at Powderham Castle.

The haunted landing at Powderham Castle with its picture of the Grey Lady.

Shillingford Abbot

There has been a settlement at Shillingford Abbot, on the south-west edge of Exeter, for at least 1,000 years. Though close to the city, the village is surrounded by beautiful farmland and the ghost stories from here are distinctly agricultural.

Another Anti-Smoking Ghost

In the 1550s in the village of Shillingford, Abbot farmers, Sir Roger de Whalingham and Sir Hugh de Creveldt were sworn enemies. After many years of bad feeling, Sir Roger, who was the elder, declared that when he died he would come back and haunt Sir Hugh three times a day. Several years later, while sitting in his armchair, Sir Hugh heard the toll of the church bell indicating that a death had occurred. The butler announced that the recently departed was Sir Roger. Sir Hugh was so pleased that he leapt out of his seat and danced around the room – until the frightened servant stammered out that the church bells were actually tolling by themselves.

Sir Hugh returned to his chair and was horrified to find a ghostly Sir Roger sitting in it. For several weeks, the ghost appeared three times a day as promised and a frightened Sir Hugh could get no rest or sleep. Then his friend Mr Izaaks arrived. He was alarmed to see that Sir Hugh looked terrible. Wearily Sir Hugh told the tale of the haunting. Mr Izaaks was sceptical and took out his tobacco pipe to mull over the information. Sir Hugh was intrigued by the new fashion for smoking and joined in. Soon the room was thick with pungent smoke. Suddenly the dead Sir Roger's voice could be heard. Shouting and swearing terribly, he vowed never to haunt Sir Hugh again.

The Interfering Ghost

Mr Court, a gardener at a large house at Shillingford Abbott, died in 1934. Unfortunately for his successor, Mr Stevens, Court's death didn't stop him from continuing the job he loved!

Stephens rearranged his shed, only to find it put back as Court had liked it the next morning. After bulbs that had been planted in a new way were ripped up, Stephens decided to keep watch, thinking, perhaps, that local hooligans were responsible. One night, to Stephen's horror, the angry looking ghost of old Court suddenly appeared in a flowerbed which had been replanted. When Stevens went out, the ghost disappeared.

The vandalism continued and Miss Walmsley, the owner of the house, who seems not to have believed in ghosts, began to blame Stephens for shoddy work. Things finally came to a head one day when Stephens was examining the results of another bout of vandalism. As he bent to smooth some trampled soil, he heard Court's peculiar laugh right next to his ear. Stephens left his job soon after.

Topsham

Located at the head of the Exe Estuary, Topsham, with its atmospheric, winding streets and lovely river views, is just 4km from the centre of Exeter. Until the advent of the railway in the 1840s, Topsham was one of England's main ports. Unsurprisingly, there are tales of several spooky seafarers!

The Banks of the Exe

In the 1600s a ship's captain from Topsham by the name of Jackson was washed overboard in the mid-Atlantic during a storm

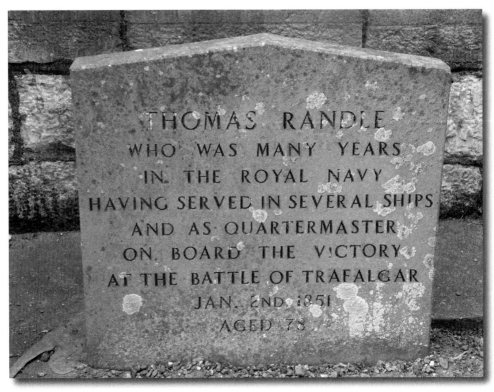

The grave of Tom Randle in St Margaret's churchyard, Topsham.

in late November. He was well liked by his crew and the Topsham community as a whole and so his loss was deeply felt. Exactly a year later, while mending nets on the banks of the River Exe at Topsham, one of Jackson's crewmen heard a familiar shout from across the river. Looking up, he saw a pale figure and recognised his supposedly dead captain. Full of joy that Jackson had, in fact, survived, the crewman jumped into a rowing boat to bring the man across. As he rowed he looked over his shoulder and could clearly see Jackson smiling and waving. Nearing the bank, the seaman looked again and saw Jackson shake his head before disappearing into thin air.

Since this time in late November, a ghostly figure has often been seen waving on the far river bank on dark nights.

The last of these, as far as I can make out, occurred in 2006 when a local sailor went to check his moorings one night before a storm.

According to 'Devon and Cornwall Notes and Queries', 1965-67, local people in Topsham often saw Tom Triman, a well-known local character and sailor, by the river working on his boat. This might not seem out of the ordinary, but Old Tom died in 1911!

A fisherman returning to Topsham late one night was startled to see flames in the night sky. They were above the boatsheds on the river. As he got closer, strange fireballs suddenly shot up into the air accompanied by horrible human screams. Thinking that people must be trapped in a burning shed, the man hurried closer. The flames and screams suddenly stopped. By the light of his powerful torch the man checked the boatsheds. There was no sign of a fire and no one else was about. Puzzled, the man told his story to another fisherman who had lived in Topsham for sixty years. The old man wasn't at all surprised, having seen exactly the same eerie sight himself. He was able to offer a possible explanation: many years before, in exactly the same spot, a boat builder and his apprentice had died when chemicals in their boatshed exploded.

Fore Street

During the 1980s assistants in several shops on Topsham's Fore Street complained that they could hear the faint mooing of cows and, worse for food shops, the smell of their dung. As there were no farm animals anywhere in the area, people were puzzled. Perhaps there was something wrong with the drains? Maybe the mooing sound was being carried on the wind? Then it was discovered that many years before a dairy was located near Fore Street.

St Margaret's Churchyard

If you climb the steps from the River Exe up to St Margaret's Church, the first gravestone you see, against the side of the building, bears the name 'Thomas Randle'. He was a seaman who served on Nelson's flagship HMS *Victory* during the Battle of Trafalgar. Legend has it that he was actually present at Nelson's death.

The ghostly figure of a man has been seen prowling round the churchyard and walking up and down the narrow street at the front of St Margaret's. The man is dressed in old-style naval uniform and points to the ground, shaking his head sadly. Locals believe that the figure is Tom Randle 'reliving' the sad death of Nelson.

Afterword

AS a writer of non-fiction, particularly in a field like history where evidence and a logical reading is important, I have always tried to keep an open mind. When I began the research for *Haunted Exeter* I must confess that this open-mindedness veered towards scepticism when it came to ghosts, poltergeists and the like. Now, in the words of the famous Monkees' song, 'I'm a believer'! So, what changed my mind?

Firstly, so many stories of hauntings and other phenomena, both ancient and modern, tie up with historical fact. Secondly, during my research I have questioned many level-headed and obviously very truthful people who have had strange experiences and then tried desperately to find logical explanations – to no avail.

Finally, I have seen, heard and felt a lot of ghostly activity which I have discussed at length with my partner Seal and other paranormal researchers. None of these colleagues can adequately explain all of them either.

Now that you have read *Haunted Exeter,* I hope it inspires you to seek out the questions and answers too.

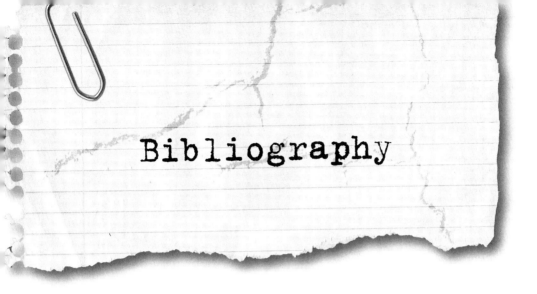

Bibliography

Books

Baring-Gould, Revd S., *A Book of Folklore* (Singing Tree Press, 1970)
Baring-Gould, Revd S., *Devonshire Character* (John Lane, 1926)
Baring-Gould, Revd S., *Early Reminiscences* (Dutton, 1920)
Curzon, F., *Lays and Legends of Exeter* (Whittaker & Co., 1851)
Gent, F.J., *The Trial of the Bideford Witches* (Edward Gaskell, 2002)
Reed, A., *Is Anybody There? Ghostly Happenings at Number 7 the Close* (2003)

Newspapers & Magazines

Exeter Evening Post
The Exeter Gazette
Exeter Herald
Exeter Weekly News
Flying Post
Westcountry Magazine; Vol. 6

Other

Devon and Cornwall Notes and Queries, Vols XXI, XXX
Devon Folklife Register, the Westcountry Studies Unit
Exeter Redcoat Guides Tour Archives
'Report and Transactions of the Devonshire Association for the Advancement of Science, Literature and the Arts'; Vols 10, 84, 105, 112, 115, 139
www.exetermemories.co.uk

Other titles published by The History Press

Devonshire Folk Tales
MICHAEL DACRE

This collection of traditional stories and tales, many of which are published for the first time, will delight lovers of Devonshire folklore. All the tales within represent this large and diverse county throughout its long and distinguished history, from the founding of Britain itself by Brute the Trojan at Totnes, to recent reports of haunted roads and phantom hairy hands. Michael Dacre has been a professional storyteller specialising in traditional tales and legends from the West Country for over twenty years.

978 0 7524 5505 1

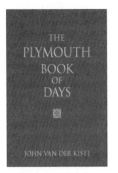

The Plymouth Book of Days
JOHN VAN DER KISTE

Taking you through the year day by day, *The Plymouth Book of Days* contains a quirky, eccentric, amusing or important event or facts from different periods of history. Find out when Plymothians elected the first woman to take her seat at Westminster, or when Laurel and Hardy made their last ever appearance onstage. Ideal for dipping into, this addictive little book will keep you entertained and informed. Featuring hundreds of snippets of information, it will delight residents and visitors alike.

978 0 7524 6080 2

Haunted Plymouth
KEVIN HYNES

Richly illustrated with over 100 pictures, *Haunted Plymouth* contains a chilling range of tales. From the ghost of Sir Francis Drake on Plymouth Hoe, poltergeist activity in one of the city's Elizabethan inns and the shade of a lady in white at Widey Court to French prisoners of war at Devonport Dockyard and a phantom pair of legs at a Mutley house, this gathering of ghostly goings-on is bound to captivate everyone interested in the paranormal history of Plymouth and will thrill all but the sturdiest of hearts.

978 0 7524 5232 6

Devon Villains: Rogues, Rascals and Reprobates
MIKE HOLGATE

Discover the darker side of Devon with this remarkable collection of true-life crimes from across the county. Including legendary north Devon highwayman Tom Faggus (featured in the classic novel *Lorna Doone*), east Devon smuggler Jack Rattenbury (known as 'The Rob Roy of the West'), south Devon murderer John Lee ('The Man They Could Not Hang'). Drawing on a wide variety of historical sources, *Devon Villains* will fascinate everyone interested in true crime and the history of Devon.

978 0 7524 6074 1

Visit our website and discover thousands of other History Press books.

www.thehistorypress.co.uk